I0845505

Printed in the United States of America.

FIRST EDITION

Library of Congress Cataloging-in-Publication Data

Risenhoover, C.C.
        The Gospel of Stupid/C.C. Risenhoover/ 1st ed.

ISBN: 9798873329618

AUTHOR'S NOTE: This is a work of opinion. The opinions are those of the author alone, although he uses quotes from other named personages to support his opinions. The author accepts full responsibility for his opinions.

THE GOSPEL OF STUPID
(a.k.a. Satan)

C.C. RISENHOOVER

BOOKS BY C.C. RISENHOOVER
Amen to Truth
Blazing Christmas
Blood Bath
Child Stalker
Dead Even
Death Angel
Fear of Truth
Happy Birthday Jesus
Hitler's Children
Hitler's Pigsty
Hitler's Seed
Hosanna to Truth
Imminent Evil
Killing Truth Softy
Larry Hagman
Legend of Henry Risenhoover
Lethal Rage
Liar, Lunatic or Lord (Ghosted)
Lying: The National Pastime
Make Some Noise
Matt McCall: An Introduction
Murder at the Final Four
Murdering America: One White Man at a Time
Once Upon a Texas Train (Ghosted)
Outside the Lines
Pedophile Pandemic
Proud to be an American
Satan D.C.
Satan's Mark
The Beauty Makers
The Suicide Lawyers
Toxic Perverts
Trashing God's Word
Trestles Over Darkness
White Heat
Winds of Truth
Wine, Murder and Blueberry Sundaes

CHAPTER ONE

"The enemy is crouching at the door" (Genesis 4:7).

In today's America a gospel of stupidity has replaced the Biblical Gospels of Matthew, Mark, Luke and John. You may go to bed at night thinking that things cannot get stupider, but when you awake, you will find you were wrong.

Neither the Democrat nor Republican Party have a lock on stupidity. No partisanship there. They are both complicit, although not equally.

However, each party, through word and deed, has defined its own stupidity.

When it comes to the amount of stupidity, bettors in Vegas do think that democrats hold a significant edge over republicans.

For example, when running for president, Joe Biden made it clear that he would reverse the Trump-era immigration policies and embrace a lenient open-borders policy.

And boy, hasn't he?

This has been one of Biden's stupider moves, and anyone with half a BB-sized brain knows it.

As a result of his open-borders policy, America has been relentlessly flooded with illegals, who are criminals, not migrants.

If you break any law, you are a criminal, so if you illegally enter the United States, you are a criminal, not an immigrant.

In October of 2023, more than 240,000 criminals crossed the border into this country. There were even more in October of 2022.

Both years were history-making. But we have not seen anything yet.

Before Biden illegally became president the highest number of illegals encountered in an October was about 90,000.

So, Congratulations China Joe, you win the lottery for releasing more criminals into the U.S. than any other American President.

For these criminals waiting to enter our country illegally, every month on Biden's border watch is sweeter than the month before.

While Biden has occupied the Oval Office, as of October 2023, some eight million criminals had entered the U.S.

To put that in perspective, the estimated population of Massachusetts is 6.95 million.

All these criminals are costing American taxpayers $451 billion annually. And funds meant for border security are being shifted to take care of these lawbreakers. The spending is unending.

New York City is spending about $10

million a day to provide shelter and services for them. And the city's mayor estimated that the city's total cost for hosting these criminals would exceed $12 billion by 2025.

And this is just one city in America.

The four Gospels of the New Testament give all people more truth than they can manage, but when people do not at least try to embrace these biblical truths, it is the epitome of stupidity.

And nowhere does Biblical truth suggest that Christians are responsible for the welfare of criminals. Yet well-meaning church members let their sympathy for the plight of these criminals override common sense.

Like everyone, I know a lot about stupidity because I have done my share of stupid things. But there's hope for a person who realizes that what they have done, or said, is stupid, and tries to correct their stupid thinking and actions.

The danger is in not being able to recognize your stupidity, or in being content with it.

It was no massive surprise to me when I awoke October 7, 2023, and learned that Hamas had, from the Gaza Strip, launched a surprise attack against Israel, committing unimaginable heinous atrocities against men, women and children.

The bitterness, hatred and stupidity Arabs have for Jews has been simmering for decades. Hatred and bloodlust are taught in Muslim schools, some run by the America-hating United Nations.

And yes, these savages mutilated, beheaded and burned babies alive. It is what Islamists do. It does not matter whether they are from Iran, Syria, Saudi Arabia, Lebanon, Iraq, Yemen, Qatar or any country where Muslims are entrenched, it is who they are. Every day they awake with the desire to kill Christians and Jews.

Let us face fact. While these alleged Palestinians are the epitome of stupidity, they are a tad smarter than those who condone what they did. And there are plenty of those in this country, especially in our colleges and universities where students and professors know a lot more about cells phones than about history, especially Biblical history.

Of course, severing the heads of Christian and Jewish babies and children is not considered an atrocity by Muslims. Islam and its Satan-inspired bible, the *Qur'an*, teach a blind hatred for both Christians and Jews, who they call infidels.

It is a stupid ideology, but we have many

politicians, media, clergy, educators and students who have never read the *Qur'an* and buy into the Islamic lies that are destroying America.

They put Islam on the same level as Christianity and are more interested in promoting homosexuality and transgender goofiness than they are in promoting Biblical truth.

This tells me that the "C" students in my high school class way back in the 1950s were a lot smarter than many of the students at Harvard and Yale today. That is because we were taught more real history than Ivy Leaguers are today.

Anyone who thinks Islam is a peaceful religion is stupid. It is a satanic evil intent on murdering every Christian and Jew on the face of the earth.

If you are not too far gone in your stupidity, worry about these savages who are crossing our southern border in droves, not so much about the Chinese and Russians whose intent toward us is more subtle and more financial.

When former President George W. Bush declared Islam to be a peaceful religion, it let all thinking people in the world know that he is not the sharpest knife in the drawer.

In fact, he is downright stupid. But could you expect anything less from a guy who is a buddy of Michele (Michael) Obama?

Two former presidents, and the current one, all of whom have even lower IQs than Bush, promote the same lie about Muslims that he does. Obviously, I am referring to Barack Obama, the only know foreigner to hold the office of president, Bill Clinton, and Joe Biden.

For those who want to punish people for the alleged sins of their ancestors, former presidents Carter, the Bushes, Clinton, Obama and Biden all had ancestors who owned slaves.

None of Trump's ancestors owned slaves. And neither did mine.

I grew up in thinking slavery and racism are sinful, and that Christians are to embrace the equality of all humankind. And I said equal, not preferred.

The Democrat Party is the party of slavery and always has been. I wonder if that is being taught in critical race theory (CRT) classes. It should be, along with the fact that after 14 centuries, Arab Muslims are still engaged in the slave trade.

As many as 180 million Africans have been enslaved in the Muslim world during the past 14 centuries. Much has been written about the Transatlantic slave trade, but little about the Islamic slave trade across the Sahara, the Red Sea and the Indian Ocean.

Whereas Arab Muslim slave trade continues today, European involvement in the slave trade to the Americas lasted for just over three centuries.

Two of every three slaves shipped across the Atlantic were men, whereas two women for every man have been enslaved by Muslims.

Almost all the slaves shipped across the Atlantic were for agricultural work, but most of the slaves destined for the Muslim Middle East were for sexual exploitation as concubines in harems and for military service.

It is a mystery to me how any black person can embrace Islam, given that Muhammad encouraged enslaving and murdering so many of their ancestors. It gives you cause to wonder why any black person would ever become a Muslim.

Could it be because they have been denied the teaching of real history in school?

Many children were born to slaves in the Americas, and many of their descendants are citizens of Brazil and the USA today. But very few descendants of slaves who ended up in the Middle East survived.

While most slaves who went to the

Americas could marry and have families, most male slaves destined for the Middle East were castrated, and most of the children born to women slaves were killed at birth.

Of the estimated eleven million Africans who were transported across the Atlantic, only five percent went to the United States. The other 95 percent went to South and Central America.

The mortality rate for slaves being transported across the Atlantic was 10 percent. The death rate for those dying in transit in the Muslim slave trade was 80 to 90 percent.

Black organizations and black politicians in the USA, along with Joe Biden, Barack Obama and politicians of every color, seemly ignore the continued enslavement of Africans and others throughout the world.

They focus on previous slavery in America, which is long past.

Although Obama's mother was white, if you think he has a legitimate birth certificate showing that he was born in Hawaii, get in the stupid line. We have plenty of people in this country who can produce a fake birth certificate, social security card and driver's license. And most of us would not know these fakes from those that are authentic.

And people in the media are among the

stupidest and easiest to fool.

So, if you swallow the lie that Obama was born in America and that Biden really won the 2020 presidential election, jump in the stupid line with all the democrats who applaud lying.

CHAPTER TWO

"The enemy is crouching at the door" (Genesis 4:7).

Following the Hamas attack on Israel and the slaughter of unarmed innocents, including babies and young children, the Biden administration sent out a tweet warning Israel not to retaliate, then quickly deleted it when they felt a little heat from people who are not so stupid as they are.

And, of course, they then said the attack had nothing to do with Biden's $6 billion dollar prisoner exchange with Iran, the leading supporter of terrorism in the world.

Right.

Just a coincidence, I guess. And if you believe that, you will believe that Bambi killed a monster crocodile, or that I had a .500 batting average in the major leagues.

But hey, let us not give Biden all the credit for sleeping with the enemy. Remember that the Ayatollah's friend, Obama, a good little Muslim, also delivered $150 billion dollars to Iran under cover of darkness.

And we are supposed to stupidly believe that all this money that is going into Iran's coffers is being used for humanitarian purposes.

It depends on what you call a humanitarian purpose. A humanitarian cause for most Muslims is the murder of Christians and Jews, all the while shouting, *"Death to America."*

In the attack on Israel, in one kibbutz forty babies were murdered, some beheaded, then mutilated, and some burned alive. That is the kind of humanitarian cause that money to Iran generates.

The Gaza Strip has always been a powder keg with a short fuse. It is the home of more than two million Palestinians. Why aren't these Palestinians living in Palestine?

Of course, that is impossible, isn't it?

How can someone be a Palestinian since there is no such place as Palestine in the Middle East?

There are, of course, thirteen towns in the U.S. named Palestine, but Gaza's residents did not come from any of those towns.

In the late 1990s, I went to Gaza to write and direct a film about the plight of children there. Because it was the only way I could get into Gaza, I went as a guest of the late Yassar Arafat, a con man and terrorist whom I despised.

If you recall, he became a billionaire on American taxpayer dollars that were sent to Gaza to help the poor. All American taxpayer dollars sent to these countries to help the poor end up, in the bank account of the country's leader.

My cinematographer and I first flew to Cairo, Egypt, then took a harrowing 100 mph taxi ride across the desert to Egyptian and Israel checkpoints at the Gaza border, dodging camel-drawn carts along the way.

The Egyptian and Israeli checkpoints were not all that far apart, but it was required that you take a bus from the Egyptian checkpoint to the Israeli checkpoint to enter Gaza.

There was an American/European bus making the short trip, also a Muslim bus. My cinematographer and I decided to take the Muslim bus to see what it was like.

We were made to wait a couple of hours before the Israelis signaled for us to board our bus and come over to their checkpoint. When we arrived at the checkpoint the guards stood around smoking cigarettes and drinking tea.

After about 30 minutes, we were sent

back to the Egyptian checkpoint because one of the Israeli guards said he did not like our Muslim bus driver.

There the bus was unloaded, both people and luggage, and loaded on to another bus. Again, we waited, this time for about an hour and a half before the bus was signaled to return to the Israeli checkpoint.

This time we sat in the bus for another 30 to 45 minutes before an Israeli guard sent us back to the Egyptian check point where everyone and everything was unloaded again, and where we switched to another bus.

More time elapsed before the bus was signaled to return to the Israeli checkpoint. By this time, the Israelis had learned that two Americans were on board, so there was no more sending the bus back to Egypt or waiting to unload at the Israeli checkpoint.

All told, it took us some seven plus hours to get from the Egyptian checkpoint to unloading our gear at the Israeli checkpoint, only a few hundred yards distance.

We discovered that the long wait was one of several ways in which the Israelis agitated Muslims. We would experience quite a few others during the time we were there.

While in Gaza, my cinematographer and I were guarded by two of Arafat's finest, each armed with an AK-47 (with no bullets).

Hamas and Hezbollah terrorist leaders were among the people I interviewed. They claimed that peace with Israel was all they wanted, but I knew their real goal is to kill every Christian and Jew to achieve it. Hatred for Christians and Jews is what they are taught from childhood.

In my interviews, I listened to lie after lie. But lying to infidels like me is taught in the *Qur'an*. It is considered a virtue, a part of the curriculum of every Muslim school.

Obama went to such a school. And Biden lies so much that he may claim to have attended a Muslim school, too, if he thinks it will get him a vote.

Of course, to some of the stupid, he could claim he came to this country on the Mayflower, and they will believe him.

What is hard for me to believe about the October attack is that the Mossad, Israel's secret service, did not know about the Hamas attack before it happened. They are one of the best intelligence operations in the world.

And Israel's borders are the most impenetrable in the world. Combined with the intelligence and military strength of Israel's Defense Forces (IDF), it is all but impossible that Hamas was somehow able to sneak into

Israel without anybody noticing.

So, for some reason was a *"stand down"* ordered that allowed Hamas to unleash terror inside Israel on October 7?

Some intelligence analysts contend that Israel's so-called intelligence failure was not an intelligence failure at all.

All Israel's border, much of which America paid for, has triple, multiple redundant systems. It is highly fortified, has state-of-the-art sensors covering every inch of it, along with troops and drills by those troops that monitor it 24/7.

If we had paid for a similar system along our southern border, along with daily troop movements there, there would be no border crisis.

Those who early on said October 7, was an intelligence failure by Israel are either lying or fools.

Conservatives tend to *"support Israel,"* believing that in its current geopolitical form it represents God's chosen people.

And Israel Prime Minister Netanyahu said that October 7, was his country's 9/11.

So, what does that mean?

Was he referring to it being a wake-up call regarding the intentions of Islam?

Some of us since adulthood, or before,

knew Islam's intentions toward us. The Muslims have not exactly hidden it, although most of our politicians have ignored it.

Well, we now know that prior to 9/11 the FBI was not allowed to investigate the terrorists who were learning to fly planes in Arizona.

Is that because they were Saudis, and some in our government have for years been trying to convince us that the Saudis are our friends?

If you buy that the Saudis are our friends, get in the stupid line.

Many people believe that the deep state, which is the intelligence community, planned and allowed 9/11 to happen.

So, does Netanyahu's statement mean Israel was in on October 7 attack.

Did Israel stand down to allow Hamas to unleash terror on Israeli civilians.

I hope not.

Dr. Francis Boyle, an American human rights lawyer and professor at the University of Illinois School of Law, has said that what Israel is doing to the people of Gaza in response to the Hamas attack on October 7, is akin to what the Nazis did to the Jews during World War II.

That is more than a bit of an exaggeration. If Israel killed every person in

Gaza, it would amount to only a little over a third of the number of Jews murdered by the Nazis.

As to why so many people in the world hate Jews, Menachem Begin, the sixth prime minister of Israel, allegedly said in a speech to the Knesset, *"Our race is the Master Race. We are divine gods on this planet. We are as different from the inferior races as they are from insects. In fact, compared to our race, other races are beasts and animals, cattle at best. Other races are considered as human excrement. Our destiny is to rule over the inferior races. Our earthly kingdom will be ruled by our leader with a rod of iron. The masses will lick our feet and serve us as slaves."*

There are those who deny Begin said this, but someone said or wrote it. And it looped back to the late Texe Marrs, an author and radio host who ran two fundamentalist Christian ministries – *Power of Prophecy* and *Bible Home Church* – both based in Austin, Texas.

And in his memoirs, former President Jimmy Carter wrote that there could have been peace between the Arabs and Israelis had it not been for the bigoted, Nazi-like racial views of Israel's Prime Minister Menachem Begin.

In a newspaper op-ed by New York public relations executive and author Ronn Torossian titled *Menachem Begin to Joe Biden: I Am Not a Jew with Trembling Knees*, PM Begin is quoted as saying to then Senator Joe Biden, *"Don't threaten us with cutting off your aid. It will not work. I am not a Jew with trembling knees. I am a proud Jew with 3,700 years of civilized history. Nobody came to our aid when we were dying in the gas chambers and ovens. Nobody came to our aid when we were striving to create our country. We paid for it. We fought for it. We died for it. We will stand by our principles. We will defend them. And, when necessary, we will die for them again, with or without your aid."*

When he was a senator, China Joe could not bully Begin, and he could not have bullied him when he was a vice-president as he bullied Ukrainian officials. Nor could he have bullied him as our fake president.

Begin, speaking to Jimmy Carter, said, *"Mister President, I wish to tell you something personal — not about me, but about my generation. What you have heard about the Jewish people's inherent rights to the land of Israel may seem academic to you, theoretical, even moot. But not to my generation.*

"To my generation of Jews these eternal

bonds are indisputable and incontrovertible truths, as old as recorded time. They touch upon the very core of our national being.

"Ours is an almost biblical generation of suffering and courage. Ours is the generation of Destruction and redemption. Ours is the generation that rose up from the bottomless pit of hell.

"We were a helpless people, Mister President. We were bled white, not once, not twice, but century after century, over and over again.

"We lost a third of our people in one generation – mine. One and a half million of them were children. - ours.

"No one came to our rescue. We were tertiated, Mister President...tertiated and decimated.

"The origin of the word 'decimation' is one in ten. When a Roman legion was found guilty of insubordination, one in ten was put to the sword. In our case it was one in three – tertiated.

"Sir, I take an oath before you in the name of the Jewish people – this will never ever happen again."

Begin is also quoted as saying, "We will defend our children. If the hand of any two-footed animal is raised against them, that *hand will be cut off, and our children will grow up in the homes of their parents."*

He also said, *"Israel will not transfer Judea, Samaria, and the Gaza District to any foreign sovereign authority, [because] of the historic right of our nation to this land, [and] the needs of our national security, which demand a capability to defend our State and the lives of our citizens."*

CHAPTER THREE

"The enemy is crouching at the door" (Genesis 4:7)

What happened in Israel October 7, 2023, and Israel's response to it, has stirred up a lot of anti-Semitism in America and throughout the world, especially on our college campuses.

But the fact that 800,000 American children go missing every year gets hardly a yawn from our legislators, the media, or on college campuses.

Anyone with half a BB for a brain knows that a vast number of these children are being used for sexual exploitation, and some for satanic human sacrifice, body parts and cannibalism. Most people do not want to even think about what some of these children are going through prior to their deaths, but they should.

Others, of course, do not care. For them it is either about money or some sort of perverse sexual gratification. The Mexican cartels have learned that the selling of children for sexual exploitation is equally, or even more profitable, than selling illicit drugs.

And if you think the homosexual agenda that is being embraced by politicians, media, educators and even clergy has nothing to do with this massive surge in child sex trafficking, get in the stupid line.

I do not know that every homosexual is a pedophile, but every pedophile is a homosexual. Queers, who once stated they were not interested in our children, now say they are coming for them.

Many of our schools, by their actions, are teaching that homosexuality and all perverse sexual activity is simply good, clean fun.

America is racing toward becoming the world's modern-day Sodom, if we are not already there. It is just a thought, but what if God no longer destroys cities for homosexuality, but just those engaged in it.

We have wasted billions on developing medicines that allow homosexuals to continue their perverse activities, money that could have been used for cancer and diabetes research.

The requirement for everyone that Joe Biden appoints to a leadership position in government is that they be anti-America, a person of color or a pervert, and preferably all three. Being qualified for the job is meaningless.

The more radically anti-America and sexually perverse a person is, the more they are treated like an endangered species.

FYI, California leads the nation in sex trafficking and Texas is second.

Percentagewise, and not surprisingly, Washington D.C. is third.

If there was a statistic for the number of pedophiles per 100,000 people, D.C. would rank first. If we were truly aware of how many legislators, bureaucrats, media, educators, judges and clergy were pedophiles, we would all be shocked from the tip of our toes to the top of our heads.

Of course, Joe Biden and Pope Francis are not the only poster boys for sexual perversion, Barack Obama did his part in loading our government with anti-America sexual perverts, terrorists and terrorist-lovers.

I do not know Texas State Legislator Matt Shaheen, who represents West Plano and North Dallas, but he and I are on the same page when it comes to child sex trafficking.

He thinks it should be a capital offense, which has always been my thinking. We should always kill evil, not simply incarcerate it where it can produce even more evil.

President Trump, too, advocates a death sentence for child sex trafficking. And, of course, all pedophiles are candidates for capital punishment.

I believe one of the major reasons the D.C. power elite hate Trump is because he was turning up the heat on child sex trafficking. Too many people in Washington are either pedophiles or making money from it.

And there is lots of money to be made.

People also to tend to forget that Massachusetts Democrat Barney Frank was allegedly running a boy prostitution ring in the halls of Congress. He was openly queer and made no pretense about it, but voters did not seem to care. He served in Congress from 1981-2013.

This is not to say Frank was a pedophile, but he was a big LGBTQ advocate, so played a large part in the government's posture toward LGBTQ, which has poisoned America's morals as much, or more, than anything else.

Shaheen is proposing the death penalty for sex trafficking a child. And he is calling on the federal government to deploy United

States special forces to Mexico to fight the cartels directly.

A lot of Texans have been calling for that, too. The cartels should be declared terrorists, because they are directly and indirectly killing more people than most of the terror groups in the world.

We have the people and expertise to wipe them off the face of the earth, so why not?

The Mexican government would not like it, of course, but what are they going to do? Most of the Mexican people are great, but their government is not our friend and never has been. They take from us, give back nothing, and are the reason for most of our problems on the border.

Biden's open borders policy has allowed thousands of criminals and terrorists to pour into the United States, along with huge spikes of illegal contraband, including an alarming increase in fentanyl.

As awful as the October 7, massacre was in Israel, in terms of numbers of deaths, it pales in comparison to the annual number of deaths the cartels are responsible for in the U.S. and Mexico.

The cartels are terrorists, and their members do not simply deserve incarceration.

They need to be put down like any rabid

animal.

When it comes to cartel sex trafficking, no 12- to 14-year-old girl is safe, nor is any younger child, male or female. Often the trafficked children end up dead when a pedophile buyer tires of them.

Thousands more end up dead from the illicit drugs that cross the border, and many Mexican people are murdered simply because of the blood lust of cartel members.

Remember this: In Mexico, most citizens do not have guns (stupid, huh?). But cartels have no shortage of guns.

Many democrats would like to put us in the same defenseless no-gun situation.

It is high time we sent these satanic cartel purveyors of evil to the pits of hell. And believe me, God will approve of it.

He wants us to destroy every vestige of evil, and we sometimes tend to forget that evil resides only in people. You cannot legislate morality, and you cannot kill evil unless you kill the people in which it resides.

So, do not be stupid. Use your brain to tell you what God wants you to do. And what He wants done is obvious to any thinking Christian.

In the face of Washington's failures, Shaheen says that Texas has an unwavering commitment to secure the border. The state's legislature has appropriated billions to that end, deploying thousands of Texas Troopers and National Guardsmen to the border to fight illegal immigration.

Shaheen says, "*We are even building portions of the wall, and Texas will continue to prioritize the safety and security of all Texans.*"

He further states that "*Even with the extraordinary efforts by our state, more needs to be done. Cartels control the northern portion of Mexico and are a clear and present danger to Americans.*

"*They have mutated from organizations focused on the sale of drugs to more lucrative lines of work such as the trafficking of people.*"

Shaheen introduced legislation, which passed, to have imprisoned sex traffickers of children ineligible for parole. As of this writing, as previously mentioned, he was working on legislation to have sex trafficking a capital offense in Texas.

Like him, sex traffickers and pedophiles deserve the death penalty, because what they do destroys lives.

And Mexican cartels have operational control of the border, only because our government allows them to have it.

In the past we sent operatives into Columbia to participate in the killing of drug lord Pablo Escobar, and Osama bin Laden was killed by Navy Seals in Pakistan.

So, we have the personnel to wipe the cartels off the map, and who cares if the Mexican government would complain about it.

The border is not just a Texas problem. It is a problem for all fifty states (although statements by Obama and Biden indicate that neither of them knows how many states make up our republic).

I doubt that geography is taught in Muslim schools.

Because of government and Christian stupidity, the enemy has already broken down the door. The door is our southern border, and it has been breached by Islamic Muslim extremists, anti-Americans, anti-Semites, drug and sex trafficking cartels, terrorists of every ilk and terrorist sympathizers.

And their invasion of America has been expedited by our government, alleged education, media and Christian aid groups.

And, unfortunately, the media has been too stupid to notice what has been, and is, happening. And, of course, many in the Fourth Estate approves of anything that destroys democracy.

In this country, people seem to be free to burn American and Israeli flags, but I've never seen a flag from another country burned.

Legitimate immigrants come to this country because they want to be Americans. The criminals who come illegally are here to destroy America.

There should be no African, Mexican, Chinese or Muslim Americans. When you leave a country, leave it. Do not bring the excrement or the flag you escaped from here. Be an American.

In 1907, the late former President Theodore Roosevelt voiced my views on legal immigrants. He said: "*In the first place, we should insist that the immigrant who comes here in good faith becomes an American and assimilates himself to us, he shall be treated on an exact equality with everyone else, for it is an outrage to discriminate against any such man because of creed, or birthplace, or origin. But this is predicated upon the person's becoming in every facet an American, and nothing but an American. There can be no divided allegiance here. Any man who says he is an American, but something else also, isn't an American at all. We have room but for one flag, the American flag. We have room but for one language here, and that is the English language...and we have room for but one sole loyalty and that is a loyalty to the American people."*

In the waning years of his life, as World War I raged in Europe and America entered the conflict on the side of the Allies, he frequently spoke of his belief that immigrants taking up residence in America should assimilate into American society as quickly as possible, learn the English language, eschew hyphenated national identities (e.g., Italian-American, Mexican-American, Irish-American, German-American, etc.) and declare their primary national allegiance to the United States of America.

Roosevelt said, *"Let us say to the immigrant not that we hope he will learn English, but that he has got to learn it. Let the immigrant who does not learn it go back. He has got to consider the interest of the United States, or he should not stay here. He must be made to see that his opportunities in this country depend on his knowing English and observing American standards. The employer cannot be permitted to regard him only as an industrial asset.*

"We must in every way possible encourage the immigrant to rise, help him up,

give him a chance to help himself. If we try to carry him, he may well prove not well worth carrying. We must in turn insist upon his showing the same standard of fealty to this country and to join with us in raising the level of our common American citizenship."

How many people in American government feel the way President Roosevelt felt. If we could find any democrat today who thinks as he did, it might fry our electrical grid.

During a Memorial Day speaking engagement in St. Louis, Roosevelt used the motto *"America for Americans,"* and declared that *"the salvation of our people lies in having a nationalized and unified America, ready for the tremendous tasks of war and peace."*

Do his words sound like Trump's to you? They certainly do not sound like Obama's or Biden's.

During his St. Louis speech, Roosevelt continued, *"I appeal to all our citizens, no matter from what land their forefathers came, to keep this ever in mind, and to shun with scorn and contempt the sinister intriguers and mischief-makers who would seek to divide them along lines of creed, or birthplace or of national origin."*

Roosevelt said he had come to St. Louis to speak on Americanism, and to condemn the use of the hyphen "*...whenever it represents an effort to form political parties along racial lines, or to bring pressure to bear on parties and politicians, not for American purposes, but in the interest of some group of voters of a certain national origin or of the country from which they or their fathers came.*"

If the former president were still alive, I know how he would have viewed the Democrat Party's anti-nationalism and identity politics. It would have sickened him, as it sickens me and all those who have not surrendered their minds to stupidity.

Roosevelt said the immigrant who did not become in good faith an American is out of place in the United States. He said the effort to keep our citizenship divided against itself using the hyphen and along the lines of national origin is certain to breed a spirit of bitterness and prejudice and dislike between the great bodies of our citizens.

My friend, the late country singer Charley Pride, once told me, "*I have been called nigger, coon, darkie and a lot of other derogatory names. Now I'm being called African American when I've never been to Africa. But all I've ever wanted to be called is an American.*"

Plain-spoken Charley made a lot of sense.

About hyphenated names, Roosevelt further said, "*This is a nation – not a polyglot boarding house. There is not room in the country for any 50-50 American, nor can there be but one loyalty – to the Stars and Stripes.*"

About immigrants, I reiterate what Roosevelt said: "*...we should insist that if the immigrant who comes here does in good faith become an American and assimilates himself to us, he shall be treated on an exact equality with everyone else, for it is an outrage to discriminate against any such man because of creed or birthplace or origin. But this is predicated upon the man's becoming in very fact an American and nothing but an American.*

"*If he tries to keep segregated with men of his own origin and separated from the rest of America, then he isn't doing his part as an American.*"

And he also said that we have room for but one flag, the American flag, and one language, the English language.

We should welcome legal immigrants, but not illegal criminals who force their way into the country under the guise of being persecuted.

We have some seventeen million of those

living in the U.S. and costing American taxpayers many billions of dollars annually. As of this writing (November 2023), more than 2.1 million of these criminals have entered the country under Biden's watch.

Joe Biden allegedly said, *"Don't compare me to the Almighty. Compare me to the alternative."*

Well, when I think of an alternative to God, I think of Satan. Is that you, Joe?

CHAPTER FOUR

"The enemy is crouching at the door" (Genesis 4:7).

After the October 7, massacre in Israel, Netanyahu said the Israelis would wipe every member of Hamas off the face of the earth. Unfortunately, that will not change much. It is impossible to destroy an ideology.

Worldwide at least 1.7 billion Islamists have been taught to hate Christians and Jews and encouraged to kill them. But for those of who understand the truth, we are accused and are supposedly guilty of Islamophobia.

The theme of most people in Gaza is *"Death to America."* So, how does our government respond to that.

We just send them more money to use against us.

That is our government's answer to everything that is Muslim and Islamic. Send them money, which they will use to kill Americans and Jews.

If that is not stupid, what is?

Democrats have benefited from the monochrome culture of college campuses. Now, however, a bill is coming due for the progressives' identification with academia.

For example, when someone says something grotesque and stupid, like praising Hamas's predatory sadism as being "*exnihilating*," you can be quite sure it occurred in academia. The butchers of the world are glorified, primarily in academia and by some media.

While many of our elected officials also love dictator assassins, they are quieter about it than students brainwashed and indoctrinated by commie professors.

Make no mistake, our government is loaded with communists, fascists, Muslims and Nazis. They are simply waiting with cowardly breath for the day that America falls, the day when they can reveal their true selves.

I am sure Obama can hardly wait for the day when he can show off his Muslim wallet with an image of Muhammad on it, probably made of Jewish or Christian skin.

And I am sure Biden sees himself as a Chinese version of Buddha.

If you are a Christian, Jew or plain old Gentile and think you are going to get a seat at the table if the Muslims or Chinese take over our country, you are thinking stupidly.

If you are a Christian or a Jew and the Muslims take over this country, believe me, you are dead meat.

And if you are not a Christian or Jew, but are willing to convert to Islam, you have the option of becoming a slave until you die.

Of course, if the Chinese take over, we all get to become slaves until we die.

This is the future of your children or grandchildren, and of all those brilliant college students who praise Hamas for killing Jews. So, be nice and give up your guns (sarcasm), which will make it easier for them.

Obviously, there is no antidote for being stupid. But a revelation may occur just before some crazed Arab cuts off your head.

Both Obama and Biden appease the Muslim world and accuse Americans who do not agree with them of Islamophobia. When towns in America begin facing the kind of savagery the Israelis face on October 7, 2023, I am prayerful that Americans will not calmly accept calls for appeasement.

But you can take this to the bank folks. If we do not wake up and combat the evil in the world, we are dead.

And that evil is Islam, Satan's curriculum and ideology for the world.

Just remember that democrats are closely connected to campuses where the only permissive ideologies are Islam, communism, Nazism, fascism, multiple genders and even more pronouns.

The Republican Party has its share of weirdness, but its stupidity stops short of sympathy for genocide, or enthusiasm for it.

Democrat stupidity, obviously, does not.

The Democrat Party seems more serious about winning and keeping power than the Republican Party. They can maintain control because so many democratic voters are dependent on the government for their livelihood.

The Democrats scratch the backs of every union known to humankind, subsidize companies that cannot make it on their own, and even fund the enemies who are intent on killing us.

And they have reaped the rewards of this generous tax-dollar *"loyalty."*

Stealing and buying votes is the Democrat modus operandi, and they feel no remorse for doing it. In fact, they pride themselves on their ability to do it.

So, I doubt that it is possible to have a truly honest election in America.

We now even have politicians from failed countries dictating our future. I have no problem with people coming to America who want to be Americans, but I resent those who come here wanting to change our country into the cesspool that they left.

And I have problems with people who were born here, who make their fortunes here, then suddenly decide that communism is superior to capitalism.

History is a great teacher, but far too few Americans know much about the history of our country or the world. We have people who want to tear down historical monuments, statues and other things that speak volumes about our history and replace them with a fictious account of the past.

These people are among the most stupid because you cannot change history, you can only learn from it.

I will never forget what my late friend Charley Pride said about history. We were at Ole Miss and a spokesperson from an NAACP contingent said, *"Oh, Mister Pride, we're so glad to have you here during black history month.*"

Charley questioned, "*Black history month? I didn't know there was such a thing. History is history, isn't it?*"

History is history.

It cannot be changed. It certainly cannot be changed by tearing down a monument or statue, or by writing a fictionalized and revised version of the truth.

Genuine history is not black, white, brown, yellow or red. Historical truth has no color or ethnicity.

If the Islamic geocidal satanic maniacs take over the earth and kill all the Christians and Jews, they still will not be able to hide God's truth, or the fact that their prophet Muhammad and the *Qur'an* was spawned in the bowels of hell.

They will not be able to hide the fact that there is no humanity in them. And they will learn the bitter lesson that the Lord God is still in control.

The alleged Palestinians can shout their slogan "*from the river to the sea*" until they are blue in the face, but it will not change a thing. The Lord God owns the universe and everything in it.

We are all just sharecroppers on God's planet.

When you have a bill of sale, you may think you have bought a piece of land, but you cannot take it with you. It remains a piece of God's earth, so no matter how much American farmland Bill Gates thinks he is buying, it will remain here after he is long gone.

Only the true God is eternal, not some pedophile and murderer like Muhammad, who conned a lot of people.

For example, the *Hadith* promises martyrs seventy-two virgins. But the word raisin and virgin are often misinterpreted as the same in the *Qur'an*.

There is, I would think, a considerable difference between a raisin and a virgin. Or in the Muslim world, maybe not.

And even if the seventy-two virgins were not a myth, what if all of them looked like Congresswoman Rashida Tlaib?

God is the only reality. We are just walking dirt until we go back to being part of the ground. And we are only walking on earth's ground for a brief period until that happens.

But do not let it to be earlier than necessary because of some blood-thirsty sword-wielding Islamic terrorist.

The 2020 census shows that 4.45 million Muslims live in the United States, up from 3.35 million in 2017. But just how many more have entered the country since Biden became president is unknown.

Because of their Islamic beliefs, these people are a danger to every American, especially Christians and Jews. What they want for America is the exact form of oppressive government that they left. They have no interest in becoming Americans, or in obeying our laws.

We have engaged in several foreign wars, but our homeland has always been protected by a couple of oceans ever since our ancestors settled here. But during Biden's tenure in office, Obama's, too, these pitiful excuses for U.S. President have imported people with murderous intent to our country.

There is no loyalty to our way of life by this imported riffraff. For many our flag is just a dust rag, or something to be burned when protesting the truth.

Wimpy, cowardly college professors, clergy and media have shattered Biblical truth with adherence to a communist ideology that has a record of failure after failure. And classrooms have been infiltrated with young people from foreign countries whose people hate us. The only real purpose of these foreign students is to poison the minds of American youth. to encourage them to share that hatred.

Our youth have been so protected from Biblical and historical truth that they cannot understand Israel's response to Muslim savagery.

They cannot comprehend 1,400 people being brutally murdered just because they are Jews. And a holocaust that took six million Jewish lives is like a fairy tale to them, or some improbable fictionalized storyline played out by Hollywood actors.

Here in America, we do not know what it is like to be surrounded by enemies, but the Israelis know.

You may recall that at the Battle of Little Big Horn, thousands of Indians surrounded General George Armstrong Custer, and we know the results of that battle.

More than a billion Jew-hating Muslims surround Israel, and it does not have oceans to protect them from the evil that is encased in the hearts of these people.

People tend to forget that most Muslims supported Hitler during World War II. In fact, Hitler's largest Waffen SS Division was comprised of Muslim Brotherhood members. And Hitler's book, *Mein Kompf*, is still one of the top sellers in the Middle East.

So, to trust a Muslim is to be stupid.

Yet Obama and Biden have placed

Muslims in key leadership roles in our government. If you are wondering why, you join a host of other people.

But people who have any degree of perception know why.

For Muslims, lying to infidels is as normal as breathing. So, if the adage *"Liar, liar, pants on fire"* were true, neither politicians nor Muslims would have any pants to wear.

And whereas the *Qur'an* teaches that lying to infidels is virtuous, democrats and most politicians think that lying to everyone is virtuous.

Baseball and football must now take a backseat to claims that they are the national pastime. That *"honor"* goes to lying.

If a democrat accuses a republican of something nefarious, you can bet it is something that the democrat is doing.

And just when you think Hillary Clinton has earned the permanent title *"Queen of Lies,"* some other democrat woman produces a whopper that knocks her off her throne.

On the male side of lying, it is equally hard to produce a clear democrat winner. Obama, Biden, Bill Clinton and RINOs Bush and Romney certainly make the playoffs. But we do not dare leave Adam Schiff off that list.

There was a clamor in D.C. that

New York Republican Congressman George Santos should be expelled because he lied about his background to get elected.

Well, he has now been expelled, but where is the outrage for Connecticut Democrat Senator Richard Blumenthal, who lied and claimed to have served in Vietnam?

So, what does that say about "*stolen valor*"? Just like John Kerry's claims about being wounded three times, lies do not count when you are a democrat.

A democrat politician could today claim that he, not Teddy Roosevelt, led the charge up San Juan Hill and he would get away with it, because the mainstream media, a subsidiary of the Democrat Party, would support his claim.

As far as mainstream media is concerned, only republicans lie, especially President Trump (sarcasm). Democrats, on the other hand, are always truthful and their motives as pure as the driven snow (more sarcasm).

Trump would have to live several thousand years and lie every minute 24/7 every day to match the number of lies that have been told about him in the past few years.

The democrat dream is to get rid of voters, and until that is achieved to control the vote through manipulation. If all genuine American patriots would simply read the

Democrat Platform, and compare it with the *Communist Manifesto*, it would have them shaking in their boots.

Unlike Israel, which is surrounded by its enemies, we have a groundswell of stupidity in our country. Our enemies are in our midst, and even sit beside us in church.

Because of our reluctance to speak up for truth and our rights, a minority of anti-America communists, Islamists, homosexuals, pedophiles and transgenders now control the majority in America.

Graduating Summa Cum Laude is no longer as important in our country as being LGBTQ+, transgender, anti-white, anti-America and anti-Christian.

Ignorance is no excuse in America. We all have access to information about what other countries and ideologies want to do to us. But stupidity reigns. People would rather watch a sitcom or football game than read or listen to the truth.

If the Islam is allowed to take over America, every known Christian and Jew will be murdered. There will be no churches or synagogues. So, obviously, there will be no celebration of Easter or Christmas.

But for those people living here who do not care and do not mind being slaves to peanut-brain murderers, there will also be no entertainment of any kind – no sports, no TV dramas or goofy game shows, no movies, no music concerts, no fashionable clothes, no elections and no vacations or time off from slave work.

I cannot adequately describe all that will suddenly be missing, including from our menus, which will be void of bacon, pork chops, pork sausage and ham.

There will be no truth or news of any kind, only a true one-party system of propaganda. And education will simply be the teaching of a murderous ideology.

But homosexuals will not be allowed to spread their anti-God rhetoric. In fact, if their sexual orientation becomes known, they will be as dead as all the Christians and Jews.

CHAPTER FIVE

"The enemy is crouching at the door" (Genesis 4:7).

Some people are so into the climate change hoax, primarily for financial reasons, that they say the Hamas attack on Israel was caused by global warming.

Is that stupid or what?

If you have a brain half the size of a BB, you will recognize the stupidity of this illogical lack of intellect. But money overwhelms intellect, and the amount of money being thrown at phony climate change staggers the imagination of most thinking people.

America is in more danger of being destroyed by phony science than by some foreign power. For decades, questionable scientific data has been used to restrict how we live our lives. And the big lie of global warming is truly the biggest hoax promoted throughout the world for the past 40 years.

Those perpetrating this hoax have stolen billions, even trillions, of taxpayer dollars. But their intent goes beyond lining their pockets with cash that rightfully belongs to you. They want to control everything about your life – the kind of house you own, lease or rent; the kind of car you drive; the schooling of your children; the food you eat and so on.

These are the same people who sought to control you with the lockdown insanity of the Coronavirus (Chinese Communist Party virus).

They invented the alleged climate virus. There is no climate crisis caused by human activities.

The climate policies of the Biden administration will do nothing for earth's climate. What they will do is create energy shortages, severely damage our economy, reduce the prosperity of every working American and make our military vulnerable as increased funds are consumed for decarbonization.

All of this is the same as a gift to China from China Joe Biden. It will give the communist regime a clear path to world domination.

We are being fed this grand delusion that electric vehicles will save the planet. Your tax money to the tune of billions of dollars has subsidized several electric vehicle manufacturers that have gone bankrupt.

Why?

Electric vehicles have been overhyped, there is a lack of natural demand, poor management, inept allocation of capital by the government, the implausibility of the electric vehicle concept, and gross overestimation of the benefits of electric vehicles reducing emissions.

Joe Biden, of course, must make everything about him. He is such a narcissist. In fact, he is a pathological narcissist from the word go and can never be sincere in his support of others.

In that sense, he is no different from Barck and Michelle (Michel) Obama, Bill and Hillary Clinton and numerous other politicians.

Like his democrat predecessors, Biden does not know how to frame issues, develop strategy, coordinate resources or execute at the tactical level.

He puts climate and equity above the needs of the American people and is adept at creating more issues than he solves. He manages issues by getting Congress to pass bills and spend money.

I reiterate, there is no global warming crisis. It is all one big scam. And the United Nations is just as adept at lying about it as Al Gore, John Kerry, Joe Biden and a host of other democrats.

The UN is a hate-America organization that we have stupidly supported with billions of taxpayer dollars.

There is no immediate human threat to the environment. It is not happening now, nor has there ever been a threat. And there will not be one in the future.

But for both fame and fortune, a scientist must now agree with the global warming fraud. There is now a climate change industry, one where scientists have become puppets of politicians and of bags filled with grant money.

If a scientist defects from the global warming lie, the truth comes at a price. He or she can lose millions in grants as well as recognition.

Our government is investigating schools for discrimination. Why not investigate them for teaching lies? Oh, I forgot, the government is the author of most of those lies.

The UN and other bodies fork out billions to organize climate change conferences, all based on lies and misconceptions pushed by secret puppeteers.

The ice mass in Antarctica is not melting; it is increasing, and there is also zero evidence that links carbon dioxide to climate change.

California's wildfires are not the result of global warming. They are the result of bad forestry management and arson.

Al Gore says the sea level will rise twenty feet by the year 2100, but real scientists, not politicians, say it will be closer to six inches. Of course, Brother Al will not be around in 2100, so he can prophesy whatever he wants about what will be happening 75 years in our future and not be contradicted.

He has asked for trillions of dollars to fight global warming, but I have yet to see how that money is going to be used. But if you followed the money, my guess is that most of it will end up in the pockets of people who have never looked at a cloud from both sides.

In other words, charlatans who are already rich, or will be when they get their hands on this money.

Global cooling is a much bigger danger to human beings than global warming.

In numerous studies done over the years, nine people die from cold for every one that dies from excessive heat. And a study analyzing seventy-four million deaths in 384 locations across thirteen countries found that cold kills twenty times more people than heat.

Going back a ways, the Ice Age in Europe from the 1600s through the 1800s caused the deaths of hundreds of thousands of people because of crop failures and famines.

And in the 1930s the *"Dust Bowl"* in this country caused 500,000 Americans to be homeless. People had to adapt to changing conditions.

The truth is that people have always had to adapt to changing conditions.

It is silly to think that humans can impact the weather more than the sun does, or the eruption of volcanos, or the ever-changing ocean currents.

The establishment, of course, does not want you to know the truth.

However, common sense plus a basic understanding of history tells you that climates in all regions of the earth continuously change over time.

Billions upon billions of dollars, maybe trillions, have been spent on alleged climate change with nothing to show for it. However, these expenditures are a politician's dream.

But saying that there is a climate crisis on earth is a false narrative being promoted by institutions like the World Economic Forum, the Vatican and the United Nations.

And a climate apocalypse is out of the question because global warming suits the earth simply fine.

So, although electric vehicles are a dismal failure, Biden puts a smiley face on every government-financed manufacturer who has flushed billions of your tax dollars down the toilet for no good reason at all.

With a straight face he tells you how more taxes and soaring utility bills are good for you. The truth is that his energy policies are devastating low-income communities throughout the United States.

Many people are hoping to get through another winter without having to choose between energy and food. They suffer off the radar of environmental activists while state and federal government impose virtue-signaling energy mandates that are futile in reducing global emissions and mitigating climate change.

The political war on coal, oil and natural gas has driven electric rates so high that many people cannot afford it. Of course, there seems to be plenty of money for the criminals (aka immigrants) who enter the country illegally, for the war in Ukraine, for Iran, and for companies willing to play the administration's climate change game.

Biden, the Senate and the House are only concerned that American taxpayers continue to pay for a bloated government. Word from all three branches of government is that they have a lot of work to do, but what they are doing is not helping you.

If I wrote about all the government waste, I would not have space for anything else in this book. But borrowing info from a newspaper column by Cal Thomas, who I read regularly, do you know that annually you are paying $196 million for the International Fund for Ireland?

That money goes for projects that include pony trekking centers and golf videos.

And last year the Pentagon announced it would spend $5.1 million to build a new golf course at Joint Base Andrews.

Like me, until I read Thomas's column,

you might not know that there are already nineteen military golf courses in the Washington area.

Another expense he mentioned was $440,000 for attendants to push buttons on automated elevators in the Capitol Hill complex; a vital and necessary function, I am sure.

The National Endowment for the Humanities spent $4.2 million to conduct a *"National Conversation on Pluralism and Identity."*

In my hometown of Jasper, Texas, we could have had this conference in the high school gymnasium, in a classroom, or over coffee in a local café, and it would have cost nothing.

And attendance would have been better, especially if the PTA sold hotdogs and soft drinks at the event.

Thomas also informed readers that the Pentagon and CIA hired psychics, hoping they would provide special insight about various foreign threats.

The cost: Only $11 million.

Did any of your local psychics see any of that money?

There was also a study to determine the quality of life in Hawaii, which only cost

$187,042. But if you wanted to know about the quality of life there, a resident would have told you for free.

Thomas mentioned $40 million in phony food stamp claims and $20 million that five Floridians stole from Medicare, part of the estimated $17 billion in annual Medicare fraud.

That is right, $17 billion.

The columnist's assessment of the situation is that members of Congress do not seem to care because it is not their money. And for them a million here and a million there is just chump change.

The current federal debt is more than $33 trillion, representing 122 percent of our gross domestic product (GDP).

American investor Warren Buffet has the answer to retiring our national debt. He suggests a law rendering all members of Congress ineligible for reelection any time the annual deficit on their watch exceeds three percent GDP.

I think most Americans would support a law like this, although we will always have the stupid among us who will vote for higher taxes and more government control of our lives.

But do you think that Congresswoman Maxine Waters, who in 2019 said that seven hundred billion people would lose their healthcare under Trumpcare, or that Congressman Hank Johnson, who said Guam might tip over if too many Marines were on one end of the island, even know that there is a GDP.

I doubt it.

It is time to say no to stupidity, and the only way to do that is to make some laws that are applicable to our Congress.

Currently, accountability is a word that has been removed from the Congressional dictionary. It is certainly a word that has been forgotten by our elected, or sometimes allegedly elected, officials.

I think many of our elected officials are illegitimate, thanks to a lot of shenanigans at the ballot box and by people we have foolishly trusted to run our elections.

Many democrats and a few republicans think cheating is simply part of the election process. And it has been for some time.

Stupid as it may sound, the votes of dead people made Lyndon Baines Johnson a senator.

And Biden was elected to the presidency by people who do not exist and others who took the opportunity to vote several times.

Here is a little tidbit for you. In the 2024

Department of Defense (DOD) budget, there is a request for $114 million for a diversity and equity initiative.

The money will be used for some sort of diversity, equity, inclusion and accessibility (DEIA).

So, what can you buy in those areas that cost $114 million? Is this the cost of some sort of policy?

It is, obviously, the cost of stupidity.

When the universities and companies that I worked for made policies, they simply sent a memo to all staff. The only expense was the cost of printed memos and secretarial time, and if the memo was emailed, there was no cost other than for the time of a secretary.

So, what about a DEIA policy that will cost $114 million?

What is happening here is the bloated cost of something like another needless bureau or division, which is unnecessary. It is just another way to politicize our military and distract it from its primary purpose.

Our military needs to be preparing for war, not worrying about how they address or respond to people in an LGBTQ or transgender cult, or women who want an abortion, or either gender who want a sex change operation at military expense.

For that matter, just how many of these people are currently in the military? I am sure they are being recruited bigtime. But I would like to know how much of the $114 million is designated to bring each normal soldier up to snuff on how they are to act toward other soldiers who are engaged in perversion, and how much is designated to enrich Biden's cronies.

And what about soldiers who joined the military and were wounded in action. Are they getting as much attention as weirdos who want a sex change operation?

I doubt it.

When it comes to stupidity, the choo-choo carrying the alleged Commander-in-Chief and all his perverted appointees, has left the track.

Do not be surprised if military medals are soon only given to soldiers based on their perverse sexual orientation. A combination of sexual orientation and race are already the primary criteria for a democrat to get a high-paying government job.

If you find that hard to believe, just check out the type of people Biden has placed in charge of our government and our military.

I reiterate that we need to pattern our military after Israel's. And instead of discouraging people from buying guns in America, our citizens should be encouraged to be well-armed, have a good supply of ammunition on hand, and know how to use their weapon.

If we keep importing criminals and Muslim America-haters, it is going to be important that all true patriotic Americans – men, women and children of age – be ready to fight for our freedom at a moment's notice.

When you analyze our current situation in the world, the only friend we really have is Israel. Most other countries are just looking for an opportunity to do us in.

That includes the Brits, who are still smarting from the ass-kicking we gave them in both the Revolutionary War and the War of 1812.

CHAPTER SIX

"The enemy is crouching at the door" (Genesis 4:7)

Because of the Biden administration's stupidity, billions of dollars' worth of our military equipment that was abandoned in Afghanistan has ended up in the hands of our enemies.

For that matter, why is some of the equipment that we provide to Ukraine sold to our enemies on the illegal market?

Not happening? Do not be naïve and stupid.

The withdrawal from Afghanistan was the right thing to do, but the way it was done was stupid, which is a trademark of the Biden administration.

Following the October 7 attack, Israel declared war on Hamas, which means that no terrorist in Gaza is safe, nor should they be. And they are terrorists, not *"fighters"* as some media insists on calling them.

A better designation for these lowlifes would be rabid animals, and their atrocities are the reason.

Similarly, it is bewildering why the U.S. has not declared war on the Mexican cartels. We should be asking why that has not happened because they, too, are rabid animals and terrorists.

Despite the hardship and hate that they encounter daily, there are a few Christians in Gaza. When I was in Gaza City, I attended the First Baptist Church (about one hundred members).

A week after returning to the states, I learned that one of its members I had met, a bookstore owner, had been murdered. I do not know how the church is faring now.

Have some Jews agitated the volatile situation in Gaza? Oh yes. When I was there trucks loaded with vegetables grown in Gaza that were being delivered to other countries were made to wait at border checkpoints until they rotted.

Some Jews hate Muslims as much as Muslims hate them.

Gaza is a hellhole and a garbage dump. In Gaza City open sewers run down the middle of the streets and into the Mediterranean where people swim and fish.

Most houses are unfinished, many with no roofs, because when a house is finished the owner must pay taxes on it. The fact is that the standard of living in Gaza makes some third world countries look like paradise.

So, why should we pay more taxes? The only thing I can figure is that democrats want more Americans to pay more taxes so they can give more money to people who do not pay taxes.

Stupid, right?

The U.S. gives the Palestinian Authority around $600 million annually, which is the same as giving it to Hamas since they control everything in Gaza.

Other countries also give money to the

Palestinian Authority for humanitarian purposes, but most of that money also goes to Hamas, into the pockets of Palestinian Authority officials, and for the purchase of weapons from Iran.

I keep waiting for our government to quit giving handouts to countries that hate us, but that is never going to happen because too many stupid people run our government.

The truth is that American tax dollars pay for most of the terrorism and wars in the world. That is whether our foreign aid goes to the corrupt Palestinian Authority or some other corrupt country like Iran that hates America.

Money released to Iran, the world's leading sponsor of terrorism, is responsible for an untold number of American deaths.

But our current government never deals with that truth.

Why?

You tell me. I just know that there is not enough soap in the world to clean the blood off the hands of the Clintons, Bushes, Bidens and Obamas.

But if you think they care, you are stupid.

While our funding of all the terrorism in the world that is raging against us is stupid, many Americans are getting rich because of it.

Terrorism and war are profitable. If you want to know who is responsible for the slaughter of innocent people, just follow the money.

Hamas and Hezbollah, like ISIS and the Taliban, are puppets. And the people operating the strings that move them may be a lot closer to your front door than you think.

Instead of focusing on gender pronoun classes, we need to focus on our ammunition shortage and the shortage of our strategic oil supply, which Biden has squandered.

The democrats want us focus on racism, hating Trump, homophobia, Islamophobia and every other phobia in the book. They want us to focus on everything other than the truth.

And when it comes to truth, we may be one of the most uninformed countries in the world. The attack on truth has reached the level of Nazi propaganda prior to and during World War II.

CHAPTER SEVEN

"The enemy is crouching at the door" (Genesis 4:7).

Many elected and appointed government officials want us to give up our guns. That is stupid thinking. An unarmed America would be a setting duck for a Muslim terrorist attack, especially since our southern border has become a sieve for illegals (criminals), including terrorists.

And again, please quit calling them immigrants as the media does. If they enter the U.S. illegally, they are criminals. American taxpayers should not be responsible for feeding, housing and educating them. Let the people responsible for this criminality take care of their physical needs.

If all government officials were forced to have one of these criminal families move in with them, how long do you think it would take to fix the border problem?

It does not require a genius to figure that out.

It also does not require a genius to figure out that the democrats do not want the border problem fixed.

Because they are giving these criminals all sorts of goodies, they are planning to also legislate that they have a right to vote.

But back to the stupid among us who want us to give up our guns. Even stupid and brainwashed terrorists prefer going up against unarmed civilians than against someone trained to use a weapon.

I read about one armed Israeli couple who killed seven terrorists during the Hamas attack October 7, saving their children from being slaughtered.

Those terrorists were not the brave *"fighters"* as some media portrayed them, unless you want to portray bravery as entering a nursery with forty children and killing them all with automatic weapons fire, knives and swords, even beheading some of them and doing obscene stuff to their bodies.

However, that is the kind of bravery these media designated *"fighters"* display. They do not attack military installations. They like to attack unarmed civilians, people without weapons who cannot fight back.

Well, do not get caught without a weapon, the knowledge of how to use it, and plenty of ammunition, because these allegedly *"brave fighters"* are coming to your neighborhood. They will soon not be crouching at your door. They will be trying to kick it in.

Even after brutally murdering innocent people, these terrorists cannot leave their dead victims alone. They desecrate their bodies. That also shows great bravery, right?

Then like dogs with their tails tucked beneath their legs, they race back to safety and use their own people as human shields against retaliation, another courageous move.

Terrorists are nothing more than minions

of Satan. He is their daddy, and they do what daddy says, no matter that it reeks of both cowardice and stupidity.

No Christian should be frightened of Satan when they have the power of Jesus Christ at their disposal, nor should they be frightened by Satan's minions, those seen and unseen.

Terrorists love to put pictures on the Internet of Christians on their knees, hands tied behind their backs, waiting to be beheaded. And they like to show the actual gruesomeness of these cowardly executions.

Terrorists murder more than 100,000 Christians every year. So, what does our government do about it?

We stupidly send the sponsors of terrorism more money, so they keep on funding the *"bravery"* of Satan's minions against unarmed people.

There are more cells of these butchers in the United States than anyone in government wants to acknowledge, thanks to non-existent border security that has evil crouching at the door of every American.

Does Biden or many of those who are in Congress care? No, not as long as they, like Judas, can keep lining their pockets with dirty money. They think they are exempt from the brutality of Islam, which is an indication of how stupid they are.

If you are a normal thinking person, you cannot understand why so many people in America want to destroy what we have. But that is because the kind of evil at your door is impossible for a normal person to comprehend.

Most Israelis, of course, have been forced to understand the evil of Islam. Jews have been dealing with it for centuries.

So, it is the height of stupidity on the part of Muslims to think they can go into Israel and murder innocent people and that Israel will not retaliate.

America, too. must learn the lesson of justifiable retaliation or face what Israel faces on a daily basis.

If we did learn the importance of justifiable retaliation, a communist organization like BLM (Black Lives Matter) and a Nazi organization like Antifa would not be allowed to commit all sorts of atrocities and never face any consequences for their actions.

Russell Rickford, a Cornell history professor is a good example of mindless stupidity. At a pro-Palestinian rally, he called the October 7, 2023, Hamas terrorist attack on Israel *"exhilarating and energizing."*

He is a typical academic weasel, out of touch with reality, who would poop in his pants if he ever had to face one of these terrorists who share his gift of cowardice.

I do not know what, if anything, Cornell will do to Rickford for his stupidity, but there were calls for his ouster. However, if the school exhibits the kind of cowardice of most institutions of alleged higher education, he will get a raise and some sort of medal.

During my years as a university professor, I was often amazed by the stupidity of some of my colleagues. Most had never served in the military and knew nothing outside of the world of academia. And most had also never worked their way through school but had gone at daddy's expense or on government grants.

And if you are a foreign student who hates America, there is plenty of free money available to you.

There are several professions requiring little or no real work, or no real thought – politics, academia, acting, media and ministry.

Many people have hidden in these areas to avoid serving in the military. You do not have to serve in the military in America, but you do in Israel. Every citizen, eighteen and over, must serve 24 to 32 months, regardless of gender or ethnicity.

America needs to follow Israel's lead on military service and on border security. Anyone with a pinch of a brain understands how stupid it is for us to fund border protection for other countries but not our own.

Thousands of military age men from Muslim countries and China are entering our country.

Ever wonder why?

When I check the alleged news daily, "*stupid*" leaps out at me from every media outlet.

And when it is impossible for people to get any stupider, I witness people believing the lies that the Bidens, Bushes, Clintons and Obamas spin.

People must be stupid or drugged to believe them.

For example, Hillary proves herself to be the perfect little communist when she tells a cable TV host, one that practically no one watches, that Donald Trump supporters need to be deprogrammed.

What she is really saying is that they need to be brainwashed.

She should know a lot about being brainwashed. She and her husband have benefitted from capitalism all their lives, amassing a fortune, but have been brainwashed (programmed) into embracing every communist despot and ideology in the world.

They may have also known more people who committed suicide under suspicious circumstances than any other couple in the world.

And they have pocketed millions from what most of us consider tragedies in the world. They epitomize the democrat strategy of never letting any tragedy go to waste.

CHAPTER EIGHT

"The enemy is crouching at the door" (Genesis 4:7).

Just when I thought things could not get any stupider, I woke up on October 5, 2023, and found that Meghan Markle planned to run for the late Diane Feinstein's Senate seat.

Meghan cannot stop thinking about how wonderful she is.

Feinstein was the richest person in either the house or senate. She had four-multimillion-dollar residences and had a Chinese spy chauffeuring her around for decades.

I am curious as to how Feinstein must feel about what I can only imagine is her current address.

The reason Meghan plans to run is because she believes it is a step toward her eventual goal of becoming President of the United States. I guess having a failed actress as president is no worse than having a failed politician like corrupt China Joe Biden occupying the office.

Either one is a travesty.

And many stupid democrats want Michelle (Michael) Obama to run.

So, let us see who we have as potential democrat presidential candidates. There's Joe Biden, of course, more corrupt than even George H.W. Bush, Bill Clinton, George W. Bush or Barack Obama; Gavin Newsome, who single-handedly has destroyed California's economy; Kamala Harris, goofy if not an idiot; Michelle (Michael) Obama; and then, of course, poor maligned Meghan.

The truth is that democrats want to get rid of voters and appoint a king or queen. Meghan has already auditioned as queen but did not get the part.

When you think of any of these clowns as commander-in-chief, you know the country is in a heap of trouble.

The possible democrats who might end up as president should have us all contacting our local bomb shelter builders.

Meanwhile, swamp behavior in Washington, D.C. goes unchecked, and we have brilliant statements from Biden like *"More than half the women in my administration are women."*

That may sound stupid to you, but with the democrat love affair with transgenderism and all things sexually perverse, they may see it as perfectly logical.

Qualifications are no longer a criterion for alleged leadership in government. A woman must be chosen, preferably a black low-information woman, and if she is a lesbian or transgender, all the better.

Sounds stupid, doesn't it?

And it is.

Most books have a theme and continuity. This one does not. I am taking the liberty of including information about various forms of stupidity at any time they cross my mind.

I was just thinking about Biden's alleged war against misinformation. He could stop a lot of misinformation if he would just quit talking, because he is the epitome of misinformation, which I refer to as lying.

You see, I prefer to call Biden's definition of misinformation what it is.

The man cannot open his mouth without lying. Of course, he and the democrats are always accusing Trump of lying, so that is exactly what they are doing. They tell on themselves.

A while back, a former university colleague complained to me that Trump was a liar. I asked him, *"What has he lied about?"*

"Everything," he said.

I responded, *"Give me an example."*

He could not. Funny. You say a man lies about everything, but you cannot cite a single example.

Joseph Goebbels was Minister of Propaganda for Hitler during World War II, but he was a piker compared to some democrats like Biden, the Clintons, the Obamas, Al Gore, Adam Schiff, Eric Swalwell, Jerry Nadler and a host of other democrats and RINO republicans.

In fact, I was going to name the *"dirty dozen democrat liars,"* but discovered naming just twelve would not do it. After compiling a list of one hundred goofy politicians and realizing I was not close to being through, I gave up.

California Congressman Adam Schiff, now running for the late California Senator Diane Feinstein's senate seat certainly stands out from the crowd.

He is not only an accomplished liar, but

also extremely stupid. And he thinks his supporters are just as stupid as he is, and he is right about that, which is one of the few things he is right about.

Despite a mountain of evidence to the contrary, Schiff still lies and claims Donald Trump is guilty of all the lies about him that were a part of the Russia hoax perpetrated by Hillary Clinton.

So, China Joe Biden is concerned about misinformation unless, of course, he is the one providing it. An interesting irony is that covert censorship is undertaken enthusiastically by those who call themselves liberal, and who claim the opposition threatens the very survival of liberal democracy.

The same folks who systematically pressured social media *"to curb the spread of misinformation"* during the COVID pandemic (Chinese Communist Virus) want to block misinformation, or what they say is misinformation, on social media like Facebook and Google.

Many in media bought and paid for by the democrats are happy to help if that *"misinformation"* is what they say it is.

For example, every major news organization except Fox News has done multiple stories on how great the economy is.

That is supposed to be truthful information. But in the eyes of voters and even government statisticians, that is a lie.

Inflation is up 16 percent and personal consumption expenditures up 25 percent since Biden took office.

No American under sixty has experienced such inflation in their adult lifetime. And because of Biden's gusher of government spending, it may be worse by the time you read this.

So, the Biden administration's truth and your truth are two entirely different things.

We, the American people, have been duped repeatedly, and by the same people. Their names and faces may change, but their intent does not.

For example, take a good look at government health officials Anthony Fauci and Francis Collins. They suppressed the theory that the pandemic resulted from a COVID virus leak from a lab in Wuhan China.

That is because they wanted to continue giving Chinese labs American taxpayer money for dangerous research. And, just maybe, they are part of the globalists who want to reduce the earth's population.

Do you think that might have had something to do with our infectious diseases gurus who recommended funding that lab with American taxpayer money? Or do you think the fact that the Bidens have been in bed with the Chinese for years had something to do with it.

It was only late in 2023 that the Biden administration suggested withdrawing funding from the Wuhan lab. We have stupidly been funding dangerous research that kills Americans and others for years.

No serial killer in history has put down as many people as the virus, yet we have people like Fauci, and the World Health Organization (WHO), want to continue funding their form of genocide.

We are not as much in danger from other countries as we are from people like Biden, Obama, Fauci, Bill Gates and the leadership of WHO. If they are so intent on saving the earth by depopulating it, why don't they volunteer to give up their lives to save it?

Or they could simply announce that they are exposing the Clintons, which would practically ensure that they would become suicide victims.

Fauci, with the aid of a complicit media, told the American people that accusing the Wuhan lab of releasing the virus was a conspiracy theory and the stupid bought it.

The stupid believe anything the government, or its cronies, say. They do not believe that *"gain of function"* research is dangerous because they are told that anything the government does is for their benefit.

Right.

And Holland was saved from flooding when a little boy stuck his finger in a hole in the dam.

Then there was the deal about masking. We were all made to think that wearing a mask and standing six feet apart would save us from the virus, whereas real research proved that wearing a mask made absolutely no difference in shielding us from the virus.

And there was never any real science behind lockdowns. The only thing we learned is that lockdowns destroy businesses and ensure that you do not have your usual company for Thanksgiving and Christmas dinner.

Sweden did not have a lock-down and had a minor increase in excess deaths compared to our 19 percent. Later research proved that lockdowns did absolutely nothing to curb the virus, but they did make Fauci a TV star.

Real scientists who disagreed with him were belittled.

Children were negatively affected by the virus because, despite it being no risk to them, teacher unions that fund the Democratic Party insisted on lockdowns and wearing masks. It was a good deal for them because lockdowns did not affect their pay.

The head honcho of the three-million-member National Education Association (NEA) teachers' union is a liberal democrat, but you would expect nothing less. The NEA is just an extension of the Democrat Party and serves no useful purpose.

Kim A. Anderson receives a base pay of $343,443, plus $82,657 taxable cash allowances. Three-fourths of the NEA staff receive six-figure salaries and forty-two receive salaries of more than $200,000 annually.

They collect dues of $375 million, much of which goes to their democrat partners in crime. No Ponzi scheme has ever been close to bilking as much money from people as the NEA.

Thanks in part to the NEA, the lockdowns resulted in a tremendous learning loss in the USA.

The American Federation of Teachers (AFT) is another union with a 1.7 million membership. Its leader is Randi Weingarten, who former CIA Director Mike Pompeo called *"the most dangerous person in the world."*

She is a Jewish lesbian who is married to a rabbi.

Pompeo said teacher unions are teaching our kids filth who do not know it is filth, while neglecting the teaching of reading, writing and math.

These teacher unions give democrat candidates millions upon millions of dollars, amounts surpassed only by the Carpenters and Joiners unions.

There are already too many homosexuals, pedophiles and Islamists teaching evil in our school systems across America. These people are a clear and present danger to our children and grandchildren. They are Satan-driven and up to no good, and you are broadcasting your stupidity if you believe otherwise.

The truth can be suppressed when the government seeks to suppress misinformation. Democrat attempts to stamp out what they term as misinformation most often turn out to be a denial of truth.

Attorney generals from nineteen states 9n 2023, along with conservative and religious organizations, opposed a Biden Administration proposal that would have prevented faith-based child adoption agencies from operating if they did not accept leftist ideology on gender identity.

The proposal would also have put children's self-identified gender identity above biological reality and would have limited family options for LGBTQ+ foster children.

The proposed rule violates religious freedom and would harm both families and children in the foster care system, but that is no big deal to Biden's bunch.

They want to remove all faith-based providers from the foster care system if they refuse to conform to democrat idealogues religious beliefs on sexual orientation and gender identity.

Biden must wake up every morning wanting to destroy Christianity and replace it with what he thinks Islam is, which it is not.

Does Islam have a foster care system?

Yes, but it is as squirrely as the so-called religion, which is nothing more than the ideology of a mentally defective terrorist. And all terrorists are as crazy as loons

CHAPTER NINE

"The enemy is crouching at the door" (Genesis 4:7).

The movie *Dumb and Dumber* seems like it epitomizes normal life today when compared to real life's stupid and stupider, especially when it comes to education, government, media, politics and even religion.

The world's stupidest people have taken control of education, government, media, politics and religion.

For example, only the stupid fail to see that pedophilia and child sex trafficking are among the major problems in the U.S. And while all homosexuals are not pedophiles, all pedophiles are homosexuals.

And education, government, media and many religionists want us to accept sexual deviancy as normal. If you follow the ideology, you will discover that most of these people are themselves deviants.

A mentally ill and deviant mind is required to accept homosexuality, pedophilia and Islam.

Most people do not want to believe there are international satanic pedophile cults in America and throughout the world whose end goal for their entertainment is the forcing and exhorting of their victims into committing suicide on live stream video.

The debauchery practiced by these rabid animals includes human sacrifice and cannibalism. They make sure that their child victims never know a minute of what straight people consider to be normal.

I will introduce you to one of these devil worshiping pedophiles who was arrested by the FBI in Astoria, New York. His name is Angel Luis Almeida, who had many sexually explicit images of himself and children.

When arrested, he also possessed firearms and was considered violent by the FBI. That takes something nowadays, especially if you are a democrat.

One of the pictures on social media was of Almeida wearing bullet-laden bandoliers and spikes in front of a flag associated with a satanic/wiccan group called *"order of the Nine Angels,"* or *"O9A."* The group is known for anti-Semitism, hatred of Christians and being identitarian (admiration for Osama bin Laden, Adolf Hitler and other despots).

O9A has roots going back to the 1960s with a stated goal of overthrowing the West's Judeo-Christian order.

Another post attributed to Almeida showed him in front of a Nazi flag wearing a shirt with the words *"Kiddie Fiddler"* on it with a caption stating that he was addicted to child pornography.

His residence was described as a horror show.

One of his posts had a satanic-Nazi flag

and drawing of a blood-soaked flaming red eyes hooded figure invoking various demons with a note stating: *"A covenant signed in blood. May the devil walk with you always-SATANE MANIBUS."*

His residence also contained the following devil worshiper books: *Lucifer Rising, Liber Null and Psychonaut: An Introduction to Chaos Magic, The Sinister Tradition: Order of Nine Angels,* and *Necronomicon.*

In June of 2022, 09A member Private Ethan Meltzer was sentenced to 45 years in a plot to kill fellow soldiers, provide material support and resources to terrorists, and for illegally transmitting national defense information to U.S. enemies.

There is no shortage of devil worshipers and pedophiles. They are legion. Among the known are 764, 676, CVLY, Court Kaskar, Harm Nation, Leak Society and H3II.

And this pedophilic cabal is continuously evolving. Cabal victims are normally in the 8-17 age group, and are most often non-straight, minorities and the mentally ill.

I daresay that anyone who chooses a homosexual lifestyle is mentally ill. The screws in their small brain have not been tightened.

Obviously, not every homosexual is a

pedophile, but every pedophile is a homosexual.

Cultists prey on children through popular games like Roblox and gaming platforms like Discord, Twitch and Telegram.

As previously mentioned, pedophilic cabal members love filmic evidence of their child victims hurting animals, themselves and committing suicide. They have methodologies to encourage them to do so.

There is an abundance of stupidity in the world today, and a real shortage of intellect. Stupidity shows up so often and so quickly that it is hard to keep up. The stupidity of today is upstaged by tomorrow's stupidity, so you cannot remember all of it. The sheer volume of it can crash the world's most sophisticated computer.

The more stupid among us ignore a rampant pedophilia and child trafficking epidemic, obsession with depopulation by so-called elites, chemtrails, alien disclosures and modified flu viruses that are unleashed on humanity by psychopathic alleged leaders who are sadistic.

And thanks to Barack Obama and Joe Biden, we have the most stupid and corrupt government (even a notch above communism) in our storied history.

Here are some of the stupid things promoted as truth by our lobotomized fake president Joe Biden and his cohorts; things that are nothing but lies and easily discerned as such by thinking people.

One of those lies is that climate change is real, caused by humans, and thus can be fixed quickly by humans.

Climate change was first called global warming by everyone running this swindle and by all those that took their bait hook, line and sinker. The suckers who took the bait would believe Nigerian scammers who tell them a distant relative they never knew died and left them millions of dollars.

Another lie they spread is that males and females can switch genders via surgery and hormone pills. But even if this were true, only the mentally ill would want to make the switch.

Still another lie is that social media is real and is especially important for social life, politics and news. This is more laughable than true.

A real whopper is that mainstream media reports the truth about war, safety and health matters. Mainstream media has sold out to communism and does only what current liberal communist government (aka the Democrat Party) wants done.

Another biggie is that all straight white people are racists, bigots, gay bashers, and hate all immigrants. If this were true, whites would have killed all people of color and homosexual persuasion years ago, and we would have an all-white world.

One of the biggest lies is that BLM (Black Lives Matter) and Antifa fight for peace, equality and human rights. These organizations promote everything but peace, equality and human rights, and are a combination of Nazism and communism.

The government promotes the lie that everything transgender and queer is good for humanity, teens, children and babies. But all they have succeeded in doing is to falsify Scripture and infect the world with AIDS, which should make the depopulation people happy.

One of the reasons that communism has gained such a stronghold in America is that most public schools instruct kids not to think. Brainwashing is real and it is on display 24/7 by alleged educators, media, government and even clergy, all of whom have taken a bite of that same fruit that Satan gave Eve.

More alleged preachers and priests are serving Satan rather than Christ but are too stupid to realize that they are mere pawns in his war against Jesus.

And the Democrat Party, the party of communism, fascism, poverty, slavery, murder and perverse sex, has become the Church of Satan.

Many people think that family tradition is more important than truth, so they vote democrat. And if that is not stupid, I do not know what is.

But how many times have you heard someone say, *"I'm voting democrat because my dad and grandad voted democrat."*

That is voting without thinking. They have no idea about what the Democrat Party has become, and really do not want to know.

A 1958 book, *The Naked Communist*, by Cleon Skousen, a former FBI employee and faith-based political theorist, exposes the plot to overthrow and control all world governments through social progressivism, and to undermine American foreign policy through internationalism (one world government) and pacifism.

The author draws particular attention to the communist goal of capturing one or both political parties in the United States. That has happened because communism has taken root in the Democratic Party, and in the Republican Party to some extent.

When you think of the Communist Party you think about a welfare state. When you honestly think about the Democratic Party, you see how they lean over backwards in their effort to create that welfare state.

Unfortunately, stupid voters never read the democrat platform. If they did, at least some of them would awaken from their lethargic stupidity.

A communist goal has been to get control of America's schools, and to use them as transmission belts for socialism and current communist propaganda.

Communists have succeeded in softening public school and college curriculum, gotten control of teacher unions and organizations, and put the party line in textbooks.

They have softly infiltrated the press, gotten control of book review assignments, editorial writing and policymaking positions.

They have gained control of key positions in radio, TV and motion pictures.

One of the communist goals is to *"support any socialist movement to give centralized control over any part of the culture – education, social agencies, welfare programs, mental health clinics."*

Another communist goal is to *"discredit the family as an institution"* and to *"encourage promiscuity and easy divorce."*

Yet another communist goal emphasized is *"the need to raise children away from the negative influence of parents"* and *"attribute prejudices, mental blocks and retarding of children to the suppressive influence of parents."*

Sound familiar?

The communist and democrat plan involves driving wedges between us based on race, income, age, gender, political affiliation and religion, all in their effort to make people view each other as enemies.

Abysmal academic performance by our public-school students is by design. This phenomenon is not new. It is often a precursor to a country becoming socialist or communist. It is called *"dumbing down"* the population because, if people are stupid, it is easy to make them believe anything.

One of the ways to get back on track is to utterly understand what our history is. Tearing down statues and revising the truth of history is stupid. History is what it is. It cannot be anything else. And real history cannot be changed.

Despite what some would have you believe; this country was founded on Judeo-Christian values and principles. Our founding document is the Declaration of Independence, and it says our rights come from God, not from government or Marxism.

The Gospels of Matthew, Mark, Luke and John are based on truth. *The Gospel of Stupidity* is based on exposing the lies that are believed by the more stupid among us. Doing that often earns a person the title of being a conspiracy theorist.

But there is nothing conspiratorial about exposing a lie.

If you are wondering why I chose the title *The Gospel of Stupid*, it is because I know that when it comes to subject matter, I will never run out of material.

Make note of the fact that increased people in today's world are following Satan, which is the most stupid thing any person can do.

And if you look closely at the word stupid, you will find lurking in the shadow images of the Bushes, Clintons, Obamas and Bidens.

They, along with quite a few others, have brought a world of stupidity down to us, all the while lining their pockets with cash.

In fact, if I focus my research on stupidity in only Washington, D.C., I will never run out of material. But since I choose to use the entire world for my sources...well, I have an infinite supply of genuine stupidity from which to draw.

In truth, my cup runs over and then some. Of course, we could blame all stupidity on this hoax called global warming (renamed climate change), which comes right out of the communist playbook.

Those of us of a more mature age remember that in in the 1970s we were being warned that we were all going to freeze to death because of global cooling

So, climate change is a subtle change of pace from that hoax.

Despite thousands of scientists telling us that global warming (climate change) is as big a hoax as the one about President Trump playing footsies with the Russians, our stupid government only acknowledges those who agree that climate change is real.

And alleged scientists who tell this lie are getting fat checks in the form of grants from our government. It is much easier to get a grant for political lying than it is to get one for telling the truth.

While climate change is stupid and unproven, legislators in Holland considered killing 200,000 cows to combat it.

Cows pass gas, so they are a danger to the climate.

So, is John Kerry a danger to the climate? He let out a big one while speaking at the big climate change circus in 2023.

And while I would miss a cow. I would not miss John Kerry.

Of course, another example of stupidity is transgenderism. It is so stupid that a man in Japan paid $14,000 to fulfill his lifetime dream of becoming a dog.

The next grandiose thing is to become a trans animal.

Why not? If a man can become a woman and a woman can become a man, what is to keep a person from becoming a dog, cat, kangaroo or alligator?

Only a lack of imagination.

The transgender agenda (and who can understand it) gets goofier and stupider every day. I guess we can blame that on global warming (climate change), too.

And we can also blame global warming (climate change) for frying the brains of so many people and making them stupid.

Honest scientists know that their global warming (climate change) predictions will not hold up. But we are told that there is an *"overwhelming scientific consensus"* about global warming (climate change).

That is simply not true.

To pursue both fame and fortune, there is a *"manufactured consensus."* Scientists have an incentive to spread alarm and exaggerate the risk of climate change because it is the pathway to fame and fortune.

Scientists, if you can call them that, who promote the global warming hoax are adopted by the environmental advocacy groups, alarmists and media and treated like rock stars. They make headlines by meetings with politicians and forecasting dire consequences if more money is not thrown up against this wall of stupidity.

If the Climategate scandal has taught Americans anything, it should be that many climate researchers are not open-minded. Alarmist scientists aggressively attempt to hide data that suggests climate change is not a crisis. This was revealed in the Climategate leaked emails.

Climategate proved conclusively that global warming is a scientific conspiracy, but the truth does not matter.

If you are interested in fake climate news, just follow the money. Alarmist scientists rake in the green while true scientists can earn only a reputation for being conspiracy nuts.

Global warming advocates, many of whom are government lackeys or media pundits, engage in a lot of covert activities, like avoiding Freedom of Information Act requests and trying to get editors fired who do not agree with them.

There is without doubt a *"climate change industry,"* set up to reward alarmism. It began with a United Nations environmental program initiated and motivated by *"anti-capitalism"* UN officials.

These people hate the oil companies, want to shut them down, and are using alleged climate change to move their policies along. If you think they are doing this to help common folk, you have bought into one of the most devious, thought-out propaganda campaigns in the history of the world.

The UN created the Intergovernmental Panel on Climate Change (IPCC). And the panel was not created to focus on any benefits of global warming. Its mandate is to look for *"dangerous human-caused climate change."*

The national funding agencies direct all funding on the assumption that there are dangerous impacts.

When has the UN ever done anything for America? The only thing they do is bleed us for more money.

Researchers quickly figured out that the way to get funded is to make alarmist claims about "*man-made climate change.*"

This is how "manufactured consensus" happens.

The editor of the journal *Science* wrote: "*The time for debate has ended.*"

So, if you want to get ahead as a scientist, receive an enormous amount of funding and be published in prestigious journals, do not question the alarmists.

To do so is a death knell for true scientists. You must agree with the alarmists if you want to be recognized and funded by our massive government-funded climate alarmism complex.

Let us get this out of the way. I am not the Q of QAnon. And my fame does not proceed me since I have none. I am just an ordinary American, and my ethnicity does not make a damn bit of difference. I do not judge people based on their skin color, but it is fine if people want to judge me on mine.

My wife is Cheyenne River Sioux (Lakota). My paternal great grandfather and my maternal great grandmother were killed by Indians but, obviously, I am not hostile to Native Americans, or I would not have married one.

An uncle died in World War I, and my father suffered three wounds in World War II, but the only German I have ever hated was Hitler, who is now busy stoking the ovens of hell.

I am extremely hostile to pedophiles and make no excuse for detesting them. I think anyone who sexually takes advantage of a little child should be hanged by the neck until dead, or have their head severed by a guillotine or dull axe.

No exceptions.

It is okay if you want to blame global warming for my attitude because, obviously, I would never be selected for a jury judging Hunter Biden, or many others of the Washington elite.

In terms of pedophilia, Jeffrey Epstein was a piker in comparison to some of our elected and appointed officials. I refuse to call them leaders.

Despite a federal investigation revealing enough evidence to put poor Jeffrey behind bars for several lifetimes, he was barely punished.

Instead of our legal establishment dismantling a major human sex trafficking network, our boy Jeffrey received only a minor penalty for sexually abusing underage girls.

He served only 13 months in a county jail and had the privilege of leaving the jail for work six days a week.

If you have a brain the size of a BB, you know why he was given this slap on the wrists. A real revelation of his crimes would have exposed numerous high-profile celebrities, politicians, judges and media people.

With his alleged suicide, Washington power brokers tried to see to it that none of the elite were exposed. If poor Jeffrey was not murdered, I am a money's uncle.

Jeffrey's client list is now being exposed. One of the names on the list is, of course, Bill Clinton. Those responsible for releasing the list had better watch their backs.

The sheer number of people who the Clintons have known who committed suicide should be in the *Guiness Book of Records*.

And, of course, many in the mainstream media are guilty of covering for more than just the commies and Nazis currently running our country.

Why did the California Assembly stupidly reject a bill to increase penalties for human traffickers? A background investigation of all those who voted against this bill would be a good place to start.

What motivated their vote? Why would any normal human being vote against such a bill?

California is, of course, a hotbed for any kind of perverse sexual activity. You name it and it is available in California.

Rampant pedophilia must not bother California Governor Gavin Newsome. I have never heard him condemn it. But most friends do not condemn friends for their transgressions.

CHAPTER TEN

"The enemy is crouching at the door" (Genesis 4:7).

A few years ago, a grieving grandmother came to my wife and I for help because the father of her grandchildren was selling them for sex to so-called elites.

She was having a tough time getting help because some of the father's clients were judges and other powerful political people in Texas.

And yes, as with the rest of the country, even in Texas there are two tiers of justice.

The father was a drug addict who was renting his children to pedophiles for $500 an hour. Fortunately, he is now dead and helping Hitler stoke the ovens of hell.

He should have been castrated, hanged and fed to some hungry feral hogs. I would have happily performed on him what should be justice for every pedophile. My wife and I felt no guilt in praying for his death.

The reason many democrats, specifically those in power, hate Donald Trump is because he would not ignore child sex trafficking while in office.

He is, obviously, a womanizer, but I do not think he has ever been accused of abusing a child. He was, however, in the process of exposing some of the major players in pedophilia in D.C. and Hollywood.

Those players have remarkably familiar names. They dominate the phony news, massaged by and for democrats, that comes from the *New York Times*, *Washington Post*, ABC, CBS, CNN, MSNBC, NBC and numerous other propaganda machines of the Communist Party.

Why? It is simple. The writers and pundits for these media are likeminded. Many are into the most perverse sexual activities known to human beings, and some in activities beyond what is known.

It has been estimated that in America 800,000 children go missing every year, and that a sizable percentage become victims of the sex trade.

Some of these children are sacrificed by satanists, witches and warlocks, voodooists and other evil cults too numerous to mention. Many are killed for their blood, which is drunk, and their organs, which are eaten.

So, the wilds of Africa and South America are not the only locations for cannibals. There are plenty of these animalistic creatures in the United States.

America has become a playground for these people if you can call them such. In my book they are nothing more than rabid animals that should be put down.

Some public schools are allowing Satanic clubs in grades as low as kindergarten. Administrators and teachers involved should be drawn and quartered. They do not need to breathe the air of normal people.

If you think Jesus would approve of what is going on in America, you do not know Jesus. If you recall, Jesus said, "...*but whoever causes one of these little ones who believe in Me to sin, it would be better for him to have a great millstone around his neck and to be drowned in the depth of the sea*" (Matthew 18:6 ESV).

Also, if you think Jesus was some shrinking violet when it came to opposing sin, read the 23rd chapter of Matthew.

Instant death is too good for these vile pedophiles. They should suffer the same agonizing deaths that they force on their victims.

I have been told that sex trafficking in America (child and adult) is a $34 billion annually industry. That is lowballing it, but I do not think I am outside the lines in saying that politicians are getting a chunk of that money.

Cartels, comprised of creatures who look like real people, become wealthy selling human beings for sex, sacrifice, blood and food.

The Department of Health and Human Services, of course, estimates that only 240,000 to 325,000 persons are trafficked in the United States annually, as if that is not enough to merit a priority for law enforcement.

Again, they are lowballing the truth.

You can pretend this is not happening, but it is going on right under our noses, and it is being done by animalistic beings that look much like normal people.

But they are not normal.

They are excrement that should be flushed from civilized society.

And we should get sick and tired of these atrocities against our fellow beings and stop them in their tracks, not tomorrow but today.

It will not be done by the scumbags in Washington who are allegedly our leaders.

They not only endorse these atrocities,

but they also engage in them.

Sex trafficking is a sinister industry that is flourishing in the hushed corners of our society. It is hidden and unspoken of, not because it is unknown, but because politicians, our legal system, bureaucrats, celebrities and media are engaged in it, or benefit from it.

Ask yourself why the Mexican drug cartels, which are also raking in billions from child and adult sex slavery, have not been declared terrorists. These cartels without provocation also murder thousands of innocents annually, and without any consequences.

The Mexican Government is just as corrupt as the Ukrainian Government. Corruption seems to be a requirement to receive American taxpayer money.

In America, people expect crimes to be exposed, prosecuted and eradicated. But when was the last time law enforcement was allowed to treat those engaged in sex trafficking, especially politicians, clergy and educators with the full weight of our legal system.

It just does not happen.

Often our police are told to stand down for fear of trampling someone's civil rights, even if that person has trampled the rights of his or her victims. But even more often they are told to stand down to ensure that no grief befalls a high-profile politician or celebrity.

Sex trafficking thrives within our borders. And each person trafficked represents a terrified, frightened captive individual forced into a life of exploitation. They are someone's child, someone's sibling. They are passed from one pervert to another, and their only future is eventual death.

God hates the traffickers and their customers. He hates sexual perversion of any kind. The trafficker and the customer will someday pay the penalty for their crime in the fires of hell, but in the meantime Christian and moral people must insist on stringent enforcement of laws that resist exploitation of our fellow beings.

We must quit standing on the sidelines and get into the game.

We must get into the game and insist on severe penalties for the wickedness that is thriving in our society today.

If you are normal, you do not understand the fascination of sex with a child. It is incomprehensible to you. It is the same thing as murder and should be treated as such.

We must revolt against the sexual permissiveness that is invading every facet of life and destroying the soul of America. It is a fight for the very essence of human dignity and freedom.

Put these human sex traffickers and their customers where they belong, standing on some gallows with a hangman's noose around their neck, or their neck in a guillotine, or their bottom in an electric chair, or standing before a firing squad.

For those who eat human flesh, drink human blood, and harvest human organs for profit, same treatment.

Too harsh? No. What is harsh is a child being sexually brutalized by an adult, their innocence destroyed, their life ruined, and often ended.

Our attitude and silence on human trafficking in this country has become a stench in the nostrils of God.

How would you feel about your son or daughter being an object for sale? When it becomes personal, people get involved. But unfortunately, when it is someone else's child, most people do not have much interest.

Well, I guarantee that with the clowns we have in office, it is soon going to be everybody's child if we do not fix the dam of depravity that is broken and on the verge of flooding the entire country.

You might want to check out who is

funding these campaigns to deride people who are attempting to expose human traffickers. The names will shock you if you can find them. The media is doing an excellent job of covering for them.

Oh well, let us just blame everything on global warming (climate change).

CHAPTER ELEVEN

"The enemy is crouching at the door" (Genesis 4:7).

If it is not already underway, while you are reading this book the globalists are eagerly gearing up to unleash another manufactured Wuhan Chinese Communist virus (COVID 19), creating a public health crisis complete with masks, lockdowns and other horrors.

Globalists love this kind of stuff. They make a lot of money doing it.

It will, of course, be a manufactured crisis completely contrived for the purpose of implementing maximum tyranny and terror on the masses, the intent being a new world order with far fewer people.

They intend to smash any means of manufacturing enough calories to keep eight billion people alive. And if they succeed, if we do nothing at all, there will be mass starvation, war and global migration.

Few realize it but we are enmeshed in a massive scientific program for total depopulation of all peoples whom the elite call *"useless eaters."* That means anyone not of slave-like use to these elite globalists.

Under the guise of fighting global warming and climate change, the globalists are systematically tearing down the current global order. They want to eradicate our large-scale agricultural systems, which are needed to keep our current population nourished and thriving.

Of course, very few of the world population are nourished and thriving, especially in third world countries.

If the one-world globalists have their way, your political affiliation will not save you. These globalist elites are coming for our children, our food and all our resources. And their intent is to shut down every form of energy.

They have already released vaccines and have blamed inferior results on global warming (climate change). They have started wars and blamed climate change. Global warming (climate change) is blamed for everything, and most people buy into it.

Why?

Stupidity.

What we have in progress is global

crime of enormous proportion, the intent being total control of the populace, no freedom, and the intent to kill millions, if not billions, of people.

We had better wake up from our slumber and be willing to fight the stupidity that has a chokehold on the world. The components of vaccines and the fear-based messaging through media is not accidental. It has been rehearsed by militaries for 25 years or more, orchestrated by people referred to as spooks.

If you comply with the tyranny of the globalists, you will end up losing your liberty and even your life.

Having a political D, I or R next to your name will not save you. Nor will your testimony that you believe in global warming (climate change). The globalists do not care about your political affiliation or anything else, only about your slave-like value to them. And if you do not have any value, you are dead meat.

What is happening in America today is the result of a movement that began in Russia some one hundred years ago. And Barack Obama stomped down on the accelerator to fast track this communist agenda in our country.

When you think of the enemy within, you

may think of Joe Biden, Nancy Pelosi and AOC, but the real mastermind is Barack Obama. At least, he is used as a mastermind by his handlers, some of the evilest people in the history of the world.

In 2008, Obama laid the groundwork for what we've seen since 2020 – the stolen election, destruction of our cities, the cozying up to BLM radicals, siding with criminals over police upholding the rule of law, championing the castration of our military, making us a laughingstock on the world stage and, along with Hillary Clinton, being the architect behind the bogus Russian collusion witch hunt against Donald Trump.

Communist and fascist leftists have infiltrated and taken over the Democrat Party. It has become even more a party of racism and hatred, attacking the foundations of our country.

Their goal is to create a one-party state and to cancel, deplatform and silence all political opponents by slandering them as white supremacists and worse. In Obama's words to *"radically transform America."*

Jason Whitlock, a black writer, wrote: *"Black elites are the true face of white supremacy. They have no interest in ending oppression. They want to benefit from it. They hate the working class and the poor. They have no moral anchor, no firm set of values. Hypocrisy is their defining moral code."*

Be aware that as Joe Biden's mental and physical health declines, the democrats will be taking some drastic steps to ensure that they (the true communist party) stay in power. Their comrade, the mass media complex, has been doing all it can to hide Joe's vast array of problems, but he is a loose cannon.

He forgets where he is, who he is, how to walk, and how to keep his hands and nose off little children.

The democrats must replace him before he is impeached, dies, or fouls up so badly on camera that the fake news cannot hide it.

Replacing him is not the problem. He is really nothing but a puppet front man for Obama, Soros, and the Chinese Communist Party. Any *'yes man'* will suffice as Puppet-in-Chief.

It just needs to be done in a timely fashion and in a way to invoke sympathy for the democrat party.

The 2024 presidential election is the most important part of this scenario, especially if Joe does not run.

Obviously, if World War III kicks into high gear, the democrats will be able to postpone the election indefinitely. They can say it is not safe to go to polling places as they did during the "*Fauci Flu Plan-demic.*"

Another scenario that is possible is that electricity and the Internet might be wiped out of service because there is an electromagnetic explosion in space that wipes out the satellites and blocks electric and Internet service for months or years.

This would keep the democrats in control during the complete mayhem that would occur – mass rioting, mass looting, murder and mass crime in all the major cities, just the way the democrats like it.

Still another scenario, Trump goes to prison before the election, which would give the democrats enough time to select another Puppet-in-Chief for their party.

Trump is also likely to be convicted. He faces ninety-one felony counts and he is being tried in districts where it is impossible for him to get a fair trial. The convictions will then be reversed after the election.

The strategy is down and dirty, unlawful convictions to influence the election, and after the election the democrats will not care if they are reversed because by that time, they will have had the desired effect on the election.

Alvin Bragg, a democrat DA, alleges

Trump falsified business records during the 2016 presidential election. And in New York they would convict a ham sandwich if it were named Trump.

The same is true in Fulton County Georgia, where another democrat DA, Fani Willis, has charged Trump with seeking to subvert the 2020 presidential election results in her state.

Then there's Jack Smith, who was appointed by the Biden administration's Justice Department. He has indicted Trump for allegedly mishandling classified material and seeking to subvert the 2020 election results.

These prosecutions, really persecutions, of Trump are not based on fair and equal justice, but on politics. If Trump were not a 2024 candidate for president, none of these charges would have been brought.

Hopefully, the American people will see through the democrat scheme. Anyone who sees this travesty of justice as anything more than political persecution should be wearing a nametag that reads "STUPID."

The reason elitist democrats hate Trump is because he was allowing law enforcement to zero in on their pedophilia. In America there are a lot more democrat pedophiles than most people can imagine. And I am sure democrats will always get the pedophile vote.

There are plenty of republican pedophiles, too, but the democrats glory and revel in sexual perversion. They want to parade it to the world, and they persecute people who will not buy into it. They even try to put a Christian spin on perversion, which is why most cannot stand the Biblical book of Romans.

The Biden administration is the most racist and sexually deviant in the history of the country. But that is to be expected since foreign-born Obama, a Muslim, is pulling all the strings on his aging puppet.

I should also mention another reason the democrats fear Trump. He is not afraid to go to prison. In fact, I think the only person who Trump fears is himself.

CHAPTER TWELVE

"The enemy is crouching at the door" (Genesis 4:7).

The democrats certainly do not want the January 6ers released from prison, because their incarceration is a primary scare tactic to keep all conservative America from rebelling against another democrat-controlled election fraud.

Fraudulent Fauci and genocide guru Bill Gates are currently working hard to find a new pandemic that can be spread by lab leaks, chemicals, mosquitos, vaccines, vax-patches, or all the aforementioned.

I heard there is a plan to use mosquitos to vaccinate people? Check it out. It is right out of the *Book of Stupid.*

Another lockdown would enable everyone who is on mandatory lockdown to vote from home and mail in their ballots. Their ballots would then be mixed in with tens of millions of falsified ballots from Communist China, just as they were in 2020.

Combine this with more flipping of thousands of votes in swing states by the alleged Soros-funded *Dominion Voting Machines* and you have yourself another stolen election, courtesy of insidious globalists, big pharma and the military industrial complex.

When I speak of military industrial complex, I am not talking about our soldiers. I am talking about those whose continued wealth is dependent on producing weapons of war.

Those of us who have sense enough to know the 2020 election was rigged are called "deniers."

I daresay that there are more deniers

than there are actual people who voted for Biden, so what does that tell you? It tells me that whatever is rotten in Denmark is beyond rotten in the United States.

Call me a denier because stupidity is required to swallow the big lie that the democrats did not steal the 2020 election. Evidence abounds that there was more fraud perpetrated than most people can imagine, but since democrats have a chokehold on the legal system and media, truth about this has about as much chance of surviving as a duck in a sea of sharks.

But getting back to the five scenarios democrats must stage, or invoke, to continue their communist overthrow of the U.S. Government in 2024. They are:

1) A Biden health catastrophe, so they can run someone like California Governor Gavin Newsome or Michelle Obama for president.
2) And if they cannot incite World War III into happening, they might stage a massive attack on the homeland that makes it seem that the war has begun so that the presidential election will be delayed indefinitely.
3) Initiate an electromagnetic pulse explosion or similar event to take down

the Internet and banking system before the election.

4) Unjustifiably imprison Donald J. Trump so that he cannot run for president.

5) Unleash a new virus or disease worse than the previous Chinese Communist Party (CCP) COVID-19, enabling the democrats to use tens of millions of fake mail-in ballots again (combined with cheating machines).

And if you think these scenarios are improbable, you do not know democrats. Make no mistake, there are numerous plans to keep these communists in power.

Call me a conspiracy kook if you like. Just remember that it is not a conspiracy if it is true.

There are more real communists in the democrat party than there are in Russia. Every law they enact comes straight out of the communist playbook.

The democrats are not only champions of pedophilia, but of all sexual perversion in the United States.

In November of 2023, investigators for the Department of Justice busted a high-end brothel network, its clientele including politicians, military officers and other influential figures.

All I can say is that if our corrupt DOJ arrested someone for selling sex it is because the brothel owners were not paying the right people.

The names of the three owners of the network are Han Lee, Jun Myung Lee and James Lee. I will leave it to you to guess their ethnicity. But I am guessing it would be no problem for the Biden Crime Family to identify their ethnicity since Hunter and Joe have been in bed with China for many years.

So, the DOJ has a list of clients of the high-end brothels – two of which were in the Washington D.C. suburbs and two in the Boston suburbs.

The Lee family charged sex buyers between $350 to $600 per hour and forced clients to fork over personal information to purchase sex, including their full name, phone number, email address, employer, credit card information, driver's license and even references.

How stupid would you have to be to provide information that could be used by a foreign government, or just an individual, to blackmail you?

It sounds to me like none of these sex clients are the sharpest knives in the drawer.

The list includes doctors, lawyers, accountants, elected officials, executives of high-tech and pharmaceutical companies, government contractors [with security clearances], professors and scientists.

And I am certain that many of these "*clients*" are among those who have voiced their concerns about Trump's previous womanizing.

Only the conservatives among these "*sex for pay*" clients face the possibility of criminal charges. Be assured that the DOJ will cover for all the democrats.

And just thinking aloud, this is valuable information for DOJ files. It is just conspiratorial theory on my part, but could not certain elected officials and bureaucrats use this information to do a little blackmailing on their own

And while initial blackmail is not always about money, it leads to money 99 percent of the time.

CHAPTER THIRTEEN

"*The enemy is crouching at the door*" (Genesis 4:7).

As I mentioned earlier, millions of kids go missing every year. Many of them are drugged, sold for any number of satanic purposes, and never heard from again.

Evil is crouching at the door of every parent in the world. Some know it, open the door and let evil in, whereas others are shocked to discover that their child is missing.

Only a ghoul wants to think about what happens to many of these children. But the truth be known, we are surrounded by ghouls and invisible demons, all courtesy of Satan.

Unfortunately, some Israelis were forced to come face-to-face with demon-possessed Gaza terrorists on October 7, 2023. And just like Pearl Harbor for us, it will be a day that will live in infamy for Israel.

As to what triggered this attack, it was nothing short of pure satanic evil. Satan has always been crouching at Israel's door, and someone opened it, or jimmied it open.

I tend to think the latter, whereas I think evil in our government has opened the door on our border to let ghouls and demons in. And we will soon pay for this stupidity with even more American lives.

Many Americans have already paid with their lives for our open border, but it is a continuing process.

The Jews fear another Holocaust, and rightfully so. October 7 was just a preview of what the Islamic world has in store for them –

bloody savagery that defies description, and many videos of the attack censored because they are too graphic of the horror that took place that day.

The ruthless and despicable way Israelis were murdered left nothing to the imagination, including babies and children being beheaded and their bodies desecrated.

Before being killed, men were forced to watch their wives tortured and raped, their helpless children brutalized and murdered in unimaginable ways.

We were given a small window into the horror of the attack, but we cannot come close to understanding how the Israelis felt who were the victims of it.

We also cannot fully comprehend how the families of the victims must feel toward Hamas.

Having spent some time in Gaza, I have a fairly good idea of how its citizens feel about the Jews.

They hate them. That is what they are taught to do. It is what the *Qur'an* teaches.

Most of the people in Gaza feel the same way about us. Like the Iranians, one of their favorite chants is *"Death to America."* And one of their favorite activities is burning the American flag.

What is our government's response to this hatred against Jews and Americans?

Just send them more taxpayer money.

And what is the United Nations response to brutal atrocities against Americans and Jews?

They are our fault.

For this response, the UN annually receives $12.5 billion in U.S. taxpayer dollars, one-fourth of the regular $50 billion in foreign aid that we shell out annually.

This does not include specific gifts to alleged allies for war, etc. As of this writing the U.S. had provided $75 billion to Ukraine, which is one of the most corrupt governments in the world.

But corruption is the criterion by which our government provides handouts.

One of my granddaughters was adopted from Ukraine, where one of my sons and his wife experienced some of that corruption in what it cost them to bring her to America.

Our government needs to wake up to the fact that you cannot buy friends. Most, if not all, foreign governments simply use us in ways it benefits them financially.

I woke up December 7, 2023, and read a newspaper story about Putin's visit to Saudi, Arabia. You know, Putin our alleged enemy and that Saudi, Arabia, the one that is laughably such a good friend to us.

You are a fool and stupider than a gazelle attacking a pride of lions if you trust anyone from the United Arab Emirates. Their friendship is based on how much oil they can sell us and how much technology they can steal from us.

They are not as sneaky as the Chinese, of course, but that is because they are not as smart. Obviously, we cannot trust China, but we sure cannot trust anyone whose believes the dribble in the *Qur'an*.

It was reported that the *"worthies"* attending the United Nations COP28 climate summit in Dubai in 2023 mostly did not eat meat.

Two key words are *"worthies"* and *"mostly."*

Meat allegedly leads to flatulence and flatulence leads to global warming. So, the summit attendees ate mostly plant-based food.

Of course, the private jets of those attending the summit emit far more CO_2 than a good steak. And, obviously, a denier like me tends to mistrust any information with a UN or United Arab Emirates stamp on it.

Shame on me.

We were told that those who attended the

summit think that our food systems are intrinsically linked to the fate of the natural world.

Various versions of this apocalyptic stupidity are emitted from every get-together of these climate conscious *"worthies"* who, despite us carnivores, are saving the world through endless talking and monies invested in this and that.

In one of his columns, Cal Thomas wrote: *"Where have we heard versions of this apocalyptic nonsense? From just about everywhere elites gather and attempt to regulate, tax us, and limit our freedoms.*

"Global warming is the secular holy of holies and those who don't embrace their faith are to be cast into the outer darkness where there is weeping and gnashing of teeth."

The elites, of course, are so much smarter than those of us who like a juicy hamburger or ribeye.

At this Dubai summit King Charles III said, *"The earth does not belong to us, we belong to the earth."*

Brilliant, huh?

We should hang on the word of every so-called royal, people who *"earned"* their title and wealth simply by being born into a certain family. And Charley boy, trained to do absolutely nothing, knows global warming when he sees it.

In 2009, when he was only a prince, he decreed (or prophesied) that we had only 96 months to avert irretrievable climate and ecosystem collapse.

So, what happened? Well, 2017 came and went with no collapse. But all climate change gurus feel compelled to predict calamity out there in the future and they can only hope people will forget their dire forecasts.

And plenty of stupid people do.

These are the same people who think Hollywood elites have some special insight into politics.

Research has shown that masking children during the COVID-19 pandemic had no real-world effectiveness, but teacher unions would still be doing it, and teachers would still be staying home if the unions had their way.

Union leaders are more interested in politics and promoting homosexuality than in teaching.

Reality for some people, especially global warming fanatics, is simply what they want it to be and what they say it is. So, they and God, obviously, cannot come to an agreement.

Anything that came out of the Dubai summit should be taken with a grain of salt, but the Biden administration will take the fantasies of the participants and try to make from them policy that will affect all of us and cost America billions.

John Kerry, one of the stars of the summit, is certainly not a climate scientist. He may know as much about the climate as our family cat, Leo, although I would not bet on it. Leo is intelligent, whereas Kerry...well, let us just say he does not light up a room with his intellect, thus making him a perfect crony for Biden.

Kerry just regurgitates what is being said by some *government bought and paid for alleged scientists*. If you believe him, you also believe Doctor Fauci, and have already bought, or have an option on, swampland in Florida.

Kerry, who failed in his effort to get three Purple Hearts for alleged wounds he received in Vietnam, is becoming increasingly militant about climate change. He sees those of us who accept the scientific fact that twenty people are killed by cold for every person killed by heat as a clear and present danger to the world at large.

Thomas wrote, *"Government leaders and bureaucrats continuously look for new crisis that will enable them to impose their will on us, although they don't obey the laws and regulations that they pass."*

And do not believe alleged *"scientific consensus."* Remember that Doctor Fauci said, *"I am science."*

What a jerk. He obviously suffers from short man syndrome.

Our government is increasingly adopting Joseph Stalin's old central planning systems of the Soviet Union. That included forced famine.

Think it cannot happen here?

Do not be so sure.

CHAPTER FOURTEEN

"The enemy is crouching at the door" (Genesis 4:7).

Following the October 7, 2023, slaughter of Israeli civilians by Hamas, there was no immediate United Nations resolution deploring the beheading, rapes and kidnappings by the terrorist group.

The UN is one of the most useless organizations on planet earth, and we should insist that they move their headquarters off American soil.

Following the attack, media, of course, was more concerned with calling Hamas *"fighters"* instead of terrorists.

If the media's definition of *"fighters"* is alleged human beings who behead babies, burn them alive and desecrate their bodies, you can call Hamas *"fighters."* I prefer to call them cowardly excrement.

In London, there was no outcry about the slaughter of Israelis. There were only protests that Israel was going to retaliate.

"Israel's at fault" many pundits say, covering up for the Islamic ideology that all Christians and Jews (infidels) do not deserve to live.

These pundits must be afraid to condemn for fear they will be put on the Islam's death wish list, which is their bucket list.

England, France, Germany, Italy and Spain stupidly opened their borders for an influx of Muslims, and they are now reaping the rewards of that stupidity.

Because of our open borders, America, too, is allowing too many of these satanic creatures into our country. Be assured they are not here to be Americans. They are here to evangelize, and eventually murder, for the cause of Islam.

Hamas, like other terrorist groups, have adopted Satan's personality.

If you have not personally met Satan, or do not believe in him, read the *Qur'an*. If you read it, and are not too stupid to comprehend what it promises Christians and Jews, you will know what Satan is like.

These Islamic demonized excuses for human beings have been trying to kill everyone who does not agree with the *Qur'an* for 1,400 years or so. And they have not suddenly given up that goal.

Because of Jesus, the Holy Spirit and the Bible, we know what God is like. So, just read the *Qur'an* and you will know what Satan is like, and you will better understand how to identify his followers.

Meanwhile, Israel's attempts to rid the world of Hamas is being blackballed by protests in the U.S. by stupid Americans and people who look a lot like those in Gaza. Most of the protester carry Palestinian flags, scream their lungs out, and look and dress like Arabs.

I am curious as to who produced a Palestinian flag since there is no country called Palestine. And I share Teddy Roosevelt's attitude about foreign flags on our soil.

They do not belong. The only flag that belongs here is the American flag, and the only people who belong here are Americans, not foreigners who want to put their country of origin first and then a hyphen before *"American."*

Those calling for a cease fire need to remember that there was a cease fire on

October 7, 2023. That cease fire ended only after Hamas attacked Israel.

If Hamas thinks they can defeat Israel militarily, its leadership is even stupider than they are.

Because of American and European stupidity about the truth, Hamas may think they are winning a PR battle. But that is because we have deranged members of our government who do not know or care how most Americans feel.

These protests of Israel's reaction to the attack of October 7, get a lot of media attention, but they do not represent how most Americans feel. A few college students and Arabs do not represent the ordinary people of America.

Rank and file Americans who are not stupid, and who have not partaken of the serpent-offered fruit, want all terrorists killed so they can live their lives peacefully.

And God wants us to kill all terrorists who have drunk Satan's venom, who like it, and who seek to destroy all decency in humanity.

Decent people lament the collateral damage to innocent people during war, but what choice does Israel have when Hamas uses innocent civilians as human shields?

Hamas sets up its evil in hospitals,

schools, mosques, etc. This speaks directly to their cowardice. Our government should be checking out what is in and what is said in the mosques in this country.

And do not be deceived into thinking that all civilians in Gaza are innocent. Most support Hamas because most hate Christians and Jews just as much as Hamas does.

If our government brings some of these people from Gaza to the United States, just remember that most of them have participated in protests where the American flag was burned, and where they chanted *"Death to America."*

We are not talking about intellectuals here.

Am I the only one who cannot help but wonder what is housed in mosques through our country, and why so many Muslims owns motels.

Could it be that the mosques are really armories for weapons, and that the motels are to house terrorists for the day when America is attacked?

Crazy, huh?

But then again, maybe not.

America has often been naïve and waited for its enemies to make the first move. This time that might well prove to be our undoing.

CHAPTER FIFTEEN

"The enemy is crouching at the door" (Genesis 4:7).

My friends Glenn and Betty Baxter have taken refuge in Costa Rica, where through books, videos and other media, they continue to warn people about the corruption, deceit, and lies that permeate the United States and Texas.

For example, they have for years been on a crusade exposing the pedophilia of high-profile people in government, education, entertainment, media and ministry earning them the title of being *"conspiracy nuts."*

Because I do not buy the party line, I am identified in the same way.

If something is true, it cannot be a conspiracy, and what Glenn, Betty, my wife and I deal with daily is truth, not fantasy, although I do author books of fiction from time to time.

Unfortunately, the truth is difficult for most people to accept. And whereas the four of us may not always agree, we can discuss any subject among ourselves honestly.

Glenn has a recent book, *Texas Under Siege*, which authenticates how Mexican drug cartels make more money from the child sex trade than from illegal drugs.

The thing I most like about Glenn and Betty is that for years they have been a large thorn in the flesh, and minds, of lying politicians, bureaucrats, celebrities, clergy, educators and media, all of whom have been engaged in both children, and for that matter, any age pornography.

And as many of you know, even being tackled and rolled into something as small as grass burrs is unpleasant. I can testify to that from my football days at our high school field in Jasper, Texas.

As for pedophilia, we all agree that every pedophile should be hanged by the neck until dead, or as Jesus said, thrown in the sea with a millstone around their neck.

That, not global warming, might cause the seas to rise, which would be good.

Glenn sees pedophilia and pornography as greater threats to freedoms in America than either Russia or China.

In fact, there's proof that China is not too much of a threat (sarcasm), since California Democrat Congressman Eric Swalwell spent a lot of time in bed with a Chinese spy, and for years the late California Democrat Senator Diane Feinstein had a Chinese driver.

Swalwell, as you recall, backed up every lie that Democrat California Congressman

Adam Schiff spoke about President Trump during the Russian collusion hoax that was perpetrated by Hillary Clinton, who the media portrays as *"pure as the driven snow."*

But Romans 3:10-12 tells us *"There is none righteous, no not one."*

And no one fulfills the truth of that scripture better than Hillary Clinton. Of course, she has a lot of competition from other politicians, celebrities, clergy, educators and media.

In his book, Glenn talks about the vile, satanic things that are tearing his native Texas apart. And the truths Glenn imparts about some high-profile people are as much in focus as a target in the crosshairs of a scope on a sniper rifle.

And he does not fire blanks.

John 8:32 tells us, *"You shall know the truth and the truth shall set you free."*

That scripture reminds me of a line from the movie *A Few Good Men*, in which the character played by Jack Nicholson angrily says to a Navy prosecutor, played by Tom Cruise, *"You can't handle the truth."*

Very few people can. Truth most often tears away the fabric of years of lies. It exposes us as the sinners that we are.

Satan, the father of lies, walks across the

land of the free and the home of the brave without encountering much opposition. And he is a welcome companion of most Americans, certainly more welcome in their homes than Christ.

But God has always worked with a remnant of people to combat Satan's lies. I know He doing a good work through Glenn and Betty.

CHAPTER SIXTEEN

"The enemy is crouching at the door" (Genesis 4:7).

Have you ever wondered why the Vatican removed fourteen books of the original Bible, especially the book of Enoch?

I am sure a lot of people have asked about that; that is, if they even knew that the books had been removed.

Most people know less about the *Bible* than they do about the birthrate of flies. They, including Catholics, also know truly little about the Vatican and the Papal support many Popes have given to some of the evilest despots in the history of our world.

Nothing is as it seems, which includes many Israelis who call themselves Jews.

My friend Glenn Baxter explains that some four hundred years before the birth of

Christ, modern day Nazis were exposed in Hebrew scripture – Ezra 2:44-58.

There is a word in these verses with which you should become acquainted. It is *"Nethinim,"* which in Hebrew means *"given."*

Nethinims were given to service in the Temple of God. They were captives and volunteers who did the work of lazy Levite priests. The Nethinims were Temple servants and were not of the House of Judah.

But they comprised almost half of the people returning from Babylonian captivity. They were foreigners who took over the House of God because of the laziness of Levite priests.

Knowing this, we can better understand why Christ said in Matthew 23, that the *"...scribes and Pharisees sit in the seat of Moses."*

The people to whom Christ referred were pure Babylonian, not Israelites. And God's people, Israel, did not care. That is why God had to go outside of his own people to find the servant and shepherd to tend to the rebuilding of the Temple.

When you understand Ezra, you will understand who had attached themselves to the tribe of Judah.

You will also better understand Revelation 2:9, concerning the Church at

Smyrna, about whom Christ said, *"I know thy works and tribulation, (but thou art rich), and I know the blasphemy of them which say they are Jews, and are not, but are of the synagogue of Satan."*

The *"cankerworm"* [Kenites] spoken of in Joel 1:4, had entered the House of Judah, and had taken over the ranking positions within the Temple and the government.

We learn in 1 Chronicles 2:55 that three families of Kenites had taken over the duties of the scribes and the interpreting of God's word.

If you want to fully explore and learn how the Kenites, modern day Nazis, are today going about destroying Christianity, I suggest you read Glenn Baxter's book, *Texas Under Siege*.

You can get a copy from Amazon or order it through any bookstore.

The population of the tiny nation of Israel is today overflowing with Kenites, and most of that population is Arabic – Crypto Jews. And spiritually they are toxic.

"They call themselves of Judah, but are not, but are of the synagogue of Satan" (Revelation 2:9; 3:9).

CHAPTER SEVENTEEN

"The enemy is crouching at the door" (Genesis 4:7).

Some people warn that we have a Sodomite Nazi government, whereas some politicians, academics, media and clergy laugh at the accusation.

But should they?

Following World War II, and with *"Operation Paper Clip,"* many of Hitler's smartest people were hired by our government and brought to America.

Do you think their ideology changed overnight?

For example, beginning with Prescott Bush, and even before, the Bushes have never been what they seemed. For one thing, Bush was not their surname in German.

It was Scherff.

George H. Scherff, who changed his name to Prescott Bush, even tried to violently overthrow Franklin D. Roosevelt in 1934. He was a banker, tied to trading with the Nazis in 1942, but by 1952 was a Connecticut Senator.

Strange, huh?

His alleged son, George H.W. Bush (George H. Scheriff Jr.), was born in 1924, and became a disputed war hero.

In late 1944, Japanese soldiers killed eight American airmen on Chichi Jima in the Bonin Islands and cannibalized five of them.

Bush was the lone survivor.

An obvious question might have to do with whether he joined the Japanese in eating his fellow airmen. The Japanese were starving, so it would make sense that their captives were starving, too.

But by 1956, H.W. was in the CIA and owned Zapata Oil (Pennzoil) Company and oversaw the failed Bay of Pigs Invasion (code named Operation Zapata).

Many say he was one of the chief architects of the assassination of John F. Kennedy, and possibly Martin Luther King and Bobby Kennedy.

He was allegedly arrested at the scene of JFK's assassination, but released

The following day, it was reported that he briefed FBI Director J. Edgar Hoover about the assassination. And Hoover, alleged to be a homosexual, certainly was not a fan of JFK.

As director of the CIA, Bush oversaw the deceptive operation of Watergate. And as chair of the Republican National Committee, he demanded President Nixon resign a day before his resignation.

Some allege that 69 days into Reagan's presidency and into his vice presidency, Bush planned and executed the attempted assassination of the president by John Hinckley.

It was reported that the Hinckley's were longtime friends of the Bushes and at one time had been next-door neighbors.

As vice president, Bush was appointed to oversee the war on drugs and deregulation, for which, along with Bill Clinton and the Medellin cartel, he pumped cocaine/crack into the U.S. through Mena, Arkansas.

It has been said that Bush fought the war in Panama simply to shut up his drug empire criminal banker, Manuel Noriega.

He is also alleged to have worked closely with Saddam Hussein and Osama bin Laden and was one of the first U.S. presidents to speak on the New World Order.

He allegedly was a top mastermind of 9/11 and helped establish the existing decades long CIA control of opium from Afghanistan.

And his deregulation of Wall Street is said to have brought on the crash of 2008.

He doubled the debt of the U.S. and, for a moment, brought democracy to its knees.

Was he, as some have said, a Nazi and a pedophile. You decide.

Otto Skorzeny was a lieutenant colonel and intelligence officer in the Nazis Waffen SS during World War II. Just before he died, he showed a picture of the Scherff family and a few friends.

Included in the 1936 picture was Mother Scherff, George H. Scherff (George H. Bush), George H. Scherff Jr. (George H.W. Bush) in a German Navy uniform, Marlin Bormann, Reinhardt Gehlen, Joseph Mengele and Skorzeny.

Bormann was Hitler's second in command. Gehlen was a chief SS officer and assassin. Skorzeny was Hitler's bodyguard and an SS/spy assassin.

Mengele, of course, was a sadistic doctor who performed gruesome operations on Jewish prisoners in Auschwitz and was known as the *"Angel of Death."* He escaped to South America following the war.

After the war, Gehlen and Skorzeny came to the U.S. in *"Operation Paperclip."* This was a program that relocated 1,600 German scientists, engineers and technicians for employment in the United States.

Skorzeny and Bush, along with Wild Bill Donovan and Allen Dulles, were instrumental in merging Nazi (SS) intelligence with the OSI to form the CIA.

There is no record that George H.W. Bush was born in the U.S. But before he died, Skorzeny said Bush had been trained as a spy and sent to America to work for Hitler, and that he was given false ID and adopted by

Prescott Bush as his son.

Stuart Smith authored a book titled *Otto Skorzeny: The Devil's Disciple* that is worth reading.

About Bush I am being sarcastic in saying, "*Just the kind of guy you want helping set up your intelligence network.*"

There is no doubt that George H. Scherff (aka George H. Bush) had strong ties through banking to Hitler and German industrialists. And it is stupid not to realize that the intelligence agencies in many countries can put together credentials that are so realistic that no one can doubt their authenticity, especially if they have as an asset their country's primary media.

For example, Obama's birth certificate and Social Security card look real.

But are they?

If not, he may well be the second, not the first, foreigner to have served as our president.

The same four groups that worked together on the Bay of Pigs plot to kill Fidel Castro may have also been responsible for the John F. Kennedy assassination.

Those groups included the CIA, with approval from Lyndon Johnson, J. Edgar Hoover, Gerald Ford and Richard Nixon; anti-Castro Cuban exiles; Mafia bosses Sam

Giancana, Carlos Marcello and Santos Trafficante; and wealthy industrialists and oilmen H.L. Hunt, Syd Richardson and Clint Murchison.

George H. Scherff Jr. (aka George H.W. Bush) had connections to all four groups.

James Files (aka James Sutton) claimed he was the grassy knoll assassin who fired the bullet that killed JFK. It is hard to find information on whether he is dead or alive. I suspect the former.

But he worked for Sam Giancana and was recruited by the CIA to train Cuban exiles for the Bay of Pigs Invasion. He claimed that one of his later advisors was Bush.

Regarding the Kennedy assassination, LBJ allegedly told his mistress, *"It was the CIA and the oil boys."*

Years ago, I had dinner with Marina Oswald, her two daughters, and private detectives investigating the Kennedy assassination.

She knew nothing, of course, but claimed her husband, Lee Harvey, was not Kennedy's assassin. I took that with a grain of salt, of course, but the private detectives laid out a compelling case for the Mafia being behind the assassination.

Jack Ruby was strongly associated with

New Orleans Mafia kingpin Carlos Marcello. Whether he worked for him or not, I do not know. I do know that they met on occasion at Campisi's Restaurant in Dallas.

The word is that Ruby was assigned to kills Oswald to keep him from talking. That is a logical assumption if the Mafia was behind the assassination.

CHAPTER EIGHTEEN
"The enemy is crouching at the door" (Genesis 4:7).

When silly Bill Clinton and his even goofier wife, Hillary, became president because of voter stupidity, and believe me when I say it was a dual presidency, communism began to rapidly thrive in this country.

It was here already, but they added coal and stoked the fire.

Hillary is a disciple of the late Saul Alinsky, and Satan. Alinsky was a Russian Jew and communist who lived in Chicago and authored the book *Rules for Radicals*.

All liberals are intrigued with dictators, possibly because they all aspire to becoming one.

Alinsky was a community organizer who lived in Chicago and, obviously, did a fantastic job there since the city has become a shooting gallery and duplicate of a third world country, just the way communists like it.

And, of course, Chicago was at one time the stomping ground for community organizer Barack Obama and his wife and/or partner Michelle (or Michael).

When Bill Clinton was Governor of Arkansas, Hillary liked to call some Arkansans *"Trailer Trash."*

But if anyone ever epitomized the definition of *"Trailer Trash"* it would be Bill and Hillary.

Collectively they have about as much couth as a rapid skunk, and morally they smell much worse.

Everything the couple does smells like corruption and immorality and usually is. If there is an honest bone in either of them no one has ever been able to find it.

When speaking about their sexual orientation, many people accuse both Bill and Hillary of being switch hitters.

That was the word on campus about him when Bill taught at the University of Arkansas Law School. It was also what I heard from the Little Rock media and law enforcement when I was a professor at Henderson State University in Arkadelphia, Arkansas.

Barack Obama continues to be a virus more deadly than the Wuhan Communist Chinese variety (COVID 19). If there ever was a charlatan and national champion liar, it is Obama.

But the Democrat Party has so many accomplished liars, it is harder to rank them than it is to rank college football teams before the season begins.

In fact, I think you will find the Top 10 impossible to rank. That is because every time you think you have a good list; you will think of another democrat who should be on it.

For example, in September of 2023, Congressman Hank Johnson (D-GA) told a reporter that immigrants are not crossing into the U.S. illegally. This is the same Hank Johnson who said he feared Guam might tip over if too many Marines were placed on one end of the island.

And, folks, he was not joking. So, Biden is not the only democrat who does not make sense.

There might even be a 10-way tie for first place.

A friend of my wife and I, a retired black female Air Force colonel, grew up in Chicago, and she knows where all the bodies are buried. She is especially knowledgeable about the sexual orientation of Barack Obama and Rham Israel Emanuel, former Chicago mayor and now ambassador to Japan.

Our friend would sooner believe that Mrs. O'Leary's cow (the one accused of starting the great Chicago fire of 1871) jumped over the moon before you could get her to believe that Obama was born in this country.

The democrats, aka the communist party, are masters at false documentation. And a phony birth certificate is child's play compared to the credentials the CIA provides for spies, or that the FBI provides for undercover operatives.

George H.W. Bush claimed to have been born in Massachusetts, but is there proof of this claim? So, I reiterate that Obama may not have been the only foreigner to hold the office of President of the United States.

While authoring this book, I read where someone, obviously on drugs, thought Joe Biden might not be a liar but simply had dementia. If that be the case, he was born with dementia because for his entire life it has been hard for him to go 24 hours without telling a whopper.

As a senator, vice president and president, he has also attempted to bully people.

Biden has always been a proficient liar, even surpassing Hillary Clinton and Barack Obama. And, yes, that sounds like an impossible accomplishment.

When democrat leadership calls Trump a fascist and Nazi, it is what they are. When they call him a liar, it is because that is what they are. When they say he will be a dictator, it is really what they want whoever they elect by hook or crook to be.

If John F. Kennedy had not been assassinated, there are democrats who would liked to have made him and Jackie king and queen.

And there are also those who would have make Obama and Michelle (Michael) our king and queen.

Try not to gag and throw up. I have already done that for you.

I am not exactly into alleged royalty. England's so-called royal family makes me want to upchuck. These are people who make no worthwhile contribution to society but live the high life on the backs of the poor.

God relented from his initial position and allowed the Jews to have a king (or that is what a prophet said), and it was downhill from there. The Jewish kings (in their minds) became more important than God.

Moses was a leader, not a king. The people had become use to being ruled by a king and dictator (Pharoah), but claimed they wanted to be free. However, when push came to shove and the going got tough, they were ready to abandon Moses and go right back into slavery.

Democrats, of course, are as delusional as these Jews were, which is why they ignore their obsession with transgenderism as if it does not exist.

It does, obviously, in less than one percent of mentally deranged men, whom the evil fairy Satan (not God) has made to think that they can be women, so they are front and center of a parade of democrats who would suck up to a maggot if it could vote.

I do not understand why these sexual deviants are so important to the racist Democrat Party since they are so few, but maybe it is because of guilt for the evil that democrats have perpetrated against minorities over the years.

Anyway, these men turned women love to participate in women's sports, probably because it is the only way they have ever been able to win a trophy. And, as you know, the democrats want to give everyone a trophy who is not a republican.

So, these men (or whatever they are), unbelievably, continue to participate in women's sports and win gold and silver medals.

Democrats shake their heads in bewilderment because, unbelievably, some democrat women are complaining about this. Some have even said it is not fair because men are much stronger and faster.

I do not know what phobia we can call this. I will leave that up to the Biden administration. Democrats downplay female concerns about competing against men by citing how few transgender men there are.

Democrat New York Congresswoman Alexandria Ocasio-Cortez (AOC) claims those who object to allowing men to insert themselves into female spaces and competitions are just looking for a way to exclude further an already *"marginalized"* group that makes up less than one percent of the population.

If you think AOC is stupid, form a line to the right. I am already at the head of that line.

That is because I am asking why 99 percent of Americans should be forced to give up their reasonable expectations of safety, privacy and fairness for the sake of a fringe minority?

Not even one female should be forced to give up her right to equal competition to accommodate the delusions of a confused bra-wearing, panty-clad man.

Democrats will say its transphobic to deny these panty-wearing men to participate in women's sports. But is not allowing it misogynistic.

Patty Sue Durdin was one of my high school classmates and the best basketball player on the girls' team. Back then women's basketball teams had six players participating in a game – three on one half the court and three on the other.

Only the three on the offensive side of the court were allowed to shoot, and none of the girls were allowed to cross the center line on the court.

Patty Sue was a heckuva shooter. She averaged over twenty points a game. She was the steady of another guy. But because we were just friends, in the summer the two of us went to the drive-in theater together every Tuesday night.

If any of the guys on our boys' team aspired to play on the girls' team, or to use their bathrooms, I am not aware of it. I do not think that any of the guys ever even thought about it.

But, of course, we were not as enlightened as people are today.

Patty Sue could shoot baskets as well as any guy, but I know she was not interested in playing on the boys' team. For one thing, she was a foot shorter than me.

My classmates also never discussed how many genders there were. They knew there were just two. Of course, we did not have any Ivy League teachers to tell us otherwise.

A new law went into effect in Montana in 2023. It rigidly defines sex in ways that Indigenous *"Two-Spirit Native Americans"* say violates their religious and cultural rights.

Montana's governor signed the bill, which defines sex as either male or female based on a person's XX or XY chromosomes and reproductive organs.

The law influences dozens of parts of the state code, including driver's licenses, demographic records and anti-discrimination laws.

David Herrera, co-founder and executive director of the Missoulian Two-Spirit Society, says, *"We do not ascribe to just simply biologic definitions. We acknowledge that there are different genders, and our cultures have always known that there are more than two genders."*

According to what I have been able to find out about this stupidity, *"Two-Spirit"* is an umbrella term referring to indigenous people who have both a masculine and feminine spirit.

I am told that historically they were assigned spiritual roles of immense importance.

Kalpana Jain, who I am told is an indigenous scholar, has written that stories passed down by the Blackfeet acknowledge and accept individual gender expression and identity because it was granted by the divine.

I plan to pass this information on to God, even though he already knows the flawed *"brightness"* of humanity that chooses Satan and hell over Him and Heaven.

What I have learned is that stupidity has nothing to do with ethnicity or color. People from all cultures have the capacity to be stupid and they exercise that stupidity on a regular basis, especially when it comes to their eternal souls.

CHAPTER NINETEEN

"The enemy is crouching at the door" (Genesis 4:7).

When it comes to gender, I suppose you can claim anything you want. The same goes for ethnicity.

Massachusetts Democrat Senator Elizabeth Warren claimed she was Native American for the purpose of getting special treatment and monies for education.

She kept this up for quite a while but was eventually exposed. If she has a thimbleful of Indian blood in her, the connection was prior to the Ice Age.

In other words, she lied. That is the criteria for being a democrat.

Unlike George Santos, a New York Republican Congressman who was expelled from the House of Representatives, she was not expelled from the Senate for lying about her background.

If all of Washington's elected officials were expelled for lying, we might lose them all, which would not be all that bad.

Like most democrats, Sister Elizabeth (not to be confused with Mother Teresa) believes that everything in life requires her supervision. Plain old Americans do not have the mental acumen to make decisions on their own. They require her help.

In other words, we are all stupid, whereas all our elected officials and those appointed by them are brilliant.

Like many whose bio lists a misspent youth and professorship at Harvard, Liz frets that the government might be missing something to govern.

In 2023, she worried that the sandwich industry might not be receiving enough government attention and supervision. That is because Roark Capital, which owns or supports various fast-food chains (Arby's, Sonic, Jimmy John's, McAlister's and Schottky's), planned to purchase the Subway chain of sandwich shops for $9.6 billion.

Liz, who is always looking out for us, immediately recognized this as a clear and present danger of a sandwich shop monopoly.

We already have *"big pharma"* and *"big tech"* that the government has difficulty controlling. Adding *"big sandwich"* might just be too much for the country to handle.

So, the good sister got a posse of Federal Trade Commission (FTC) folks together to, hopefully, help her styme this monopoly before it could get started.

If you recall, Liz initiated legislation that has made buying a house an ordeal, making sure the government controlled all facets of it to the chagrin of buyers, sellers, realtors, lenders and even the Chinese market place for American bats and dogs.

I am sure government control of the sandwich industry will have far-reaching effects, even to the policing of mothers who prepare school lunches for their kids.

My wife and I stand accused of breaking child labor laws because whenever our six-year-old grandson likes, we allow him to make his own sandwich, which, surprisingly, he can do without government supervision.

Fast food places already pay a tax on sandwiches that they sell to customers, but the Biden administration may soon also want to tax sandwiches made in the home.

And I can see Biden making Liz the *"Sandwich Czar,"* which would look good on her resume." That could very well lead to the FTC by semantic fiat reducing the number of sandwich shops across America.

For your information, Obama appointed fifty czars and George W. Bush appointed forty-nine. We have yet to see how many Biden will appoint.

But I am surprised that our Congress has not already debated and made laws about sandwiches. From what I understand sandwiches contribute to global warming. They are loaded with CO2.

The FTC is open to legislation that decrees a sandwich made of beef or chicken is not a sandwich unless it is served cold. This is good news since most of us prefer that the meat on our hamburgers be hot.

People are tired of Congress debating unimportant stuff like our border crisis, national debt, and how much money we should send to Israel and Ukraine with which to conduct their wars.

We need to deal with the threat of a sandwich monopoly, and we need to do it now. And we must get down to the basics, like the definition of a sandwich that every American can understand.

CHAPTER TWENTY

"The enemy is crouching at the door" (Genesis 4:7).

Hopefully, you know I am being sarcastic, and that like me you think worrying about a sandwich monopoly is stupid. But what is even more stupid is the proclamations that came out of the COP28 conference in Dubai in 2023.

Drum roll, please.

The Biden administration made two oh so virtuous proclamations that it says will help save the planet from climate change.

Neither of these proclamations will, of course, change the planet's temperature by even one-tenth of a percent, but they might well destroy the 21st-century American economy as we know it.

Team Biden first announced that it will stop production of all new coal plants in the United States, which comes on the heels of Biden's Environmental Protection Agency (EPA) saying that this year it would impose new power plant emission regulations, the compliance of which will be all but impossible for coal plants to follow.

Brilliant, right?

But that is just the beginning. The next day VP Kamala Harris proclaimed new rules to sharply reduce methane from the oil and natural gas industry.

White House geniuses call methane a super-pollutant that they want to eliminate because it is many times more powerful than carbon dioxide.

But wait, I am puzzled. Isn't methane effectively a hydrocarbon that comes from natural gas, something most of us learned in high school science class?

So, is not eliminating methane also a ban on natural-gas power plants.

Eradicating coal and natural-gas plants will ravage America's electric power capacity, causing blackouts and brownouts across the country, a forerunner of radical anti-fossil fuel policies.

Of course, the lights will still be on in the White House, just not in your house. Electricity for home heating in winter and for cooling in the summer will have to be turned off or rationed.

Hospitals, schools, the internet, construction projects and factories will routinely be shut down when unreliable alternative energy like wind and solar power cannot deliver the power they need.

So, we will be sitting ducks for every dictatorship in the world, which must sound wonderful to anti-Americans like Biden and Obama.

Is China following the energy lead of our maniacal government?

Is Russia?

These are elementary easy-to-answer questions. And they have the entire world asking, *"Is Biden stupid?"*

You know the answer to that as well as I do.

If America is forced to follow this clown's leadership, 60 percent of our country's electric—power generation will go away; and sooner than we think.

Currently coal provides 20 percent of our electric power and natural gas supplies about 40 percent.

I simply question that if most, or all, of our population dies in our efforts to avert alleged global warming, for whom are we saving the planet?

China?

Or we are saving it for the Muslim world, people who were walking around with a pan catching camel droppings with which to build a fire until we discovered oil for them and insisted on paying a fortune for it.

Feel stupid yet?

How are we going to make up for the loss of 60 percent or more of our electric power? Unless people like Bill Gates can depopulate the earth, and soon, more people mean more demand for electricity.

We now have a bunch of idiots who want all vehicles to be powered up on the electric grid, while all the while destroying the resources for that grid.

If you have more than a half BB-sized brain, you realize how stupid this is. Biden, a standard bearer for stupidity, has assembled an administration that is not as smart as he is, which took some doing.

That should make us afraid. Very afraid.

Stephen Moore, a senior fellow at the Heritage Foundation, and one of my favorite newspaper columnists, wrote: *"Some people may believe these mandatory sacrifices and rationing of modern-age conveniences are justified to stave off 'catastrophic climate change.'*

"*Except the shutdown of our coal and natural-gas power plants will not move the needle a millimeter on greenhouse gas emissions – and may make global CO2 emissions worse, not better.*

"*That's because by far the biggest emitter of greenhouse gas emissions – China – isn't playing in this climate-change sandbox.*"

Moore does not outright call Biden and his climate czar, John Kerry, dumb and dumber, so I will do that for him, and for all Americans who are not brain dead.

Moore further wrote: "*The coal plants and mines we shut down in places like Pennsylvania, West Virginia and Wyoming are being replaced two or three times over by newly built coal fire plants in India and China.*

"*We shut down one plant; they bring on line two or three new ones.*

"*The math does not add up – especially since we have cleaner coal plants than China does.*

"*Biden is playing a dangerous game of unilateral disarmament.*

"If he has his way, we will jump off the cliff first in the naïve hope that China, India, Russia and Europe are right behind us."

Biden is, of course, in a delusionary state if he thinks anyone with a brain is going to follow him in anything. All world leaders are bewildered that the buffoon was elected president, but most know it was only because of a rigged election.

People who do not genuinely fear Biden's stupidity are stupid. But by late 2023, he had appointed more judges to federal courts than any president since John F. Kennedy.

Among those appointed are a record number of women and racial and ethnic minorities. Obviously, many of these people are not qualified, because Biden has proven that being qualified is not a requirement for any of his appointees; his only criteria being that they be out of the mainstream mentally, sexually, or both.

This should make you wonder what goes on in the privacy of the White House.

CHAPTER TWENTY-ONE

"The enemy is crouching at the door" (Genesis 4:7).

Lying and politics go together like a hand in a glove. I do not know if anyone in public office has cheated or lied to get there. However, very few politicians have ever been punished for their lying.

Republicans who lie are always exposed. Democrats who lie are always applauded, especially by their silly and complicit media.

George Santos, a republican from New York, lied about his background, which may or may not have been the reason he was elected to the U.S. House of Representatives.

Regardless, fellow republicans, with help from joyful democrats, expelled him from his elected seat on the pretense that it was because of his lying.

You do not have to be one of God's right-hand men to know that everyone who voted to expel George for his lying is a liar.

We all lie from time to time, often attributing our lies to ignorance. We even label some lies as being innocent. But there is no such thing as an innocent lie.

Sister Elizabeth Warren, who may someday become America's first *"sandwich czar,"* or may already be by the time you read this book, lied about her heritage.

Democrat Senator Richard Blumenthal lied about being in Vietnam.

Democrat John Kerry lied about his heroics and wounds in Vietnam.

Biden, Obama, George W. Bush, Bill and Hillary Clinton, Jamaal Bowman, Adam Schiff and Eric Swalwell lie about everything.

And if you are wondering about Bush being included in this tribe of goats, he is really a democrat. He just played republican for a time to spy on the Republican Party, just as his daddy was alleged to be a spy for Hitler before and during World War II.

Some people admire and idolize these miscreants, but it will be a freezing day in hell before I give hero status to a politician. If they are not vermin, they are on their way to being even worse. So, if one of them was on fire, I would not use my urine to put it out.

Bitter? You bet. But not stupid enough to buy the excrement the democrats are selling.

I am not a Santos fan, but he is just as worthy of his former post as most lying democrats who remain in Congress.

House democrats allowed their comrade, Eric Swalwell of California, to remain chair of the House Foreign Relations Committee, even after revelations that he was having an affair with a Chinese spy. And they blocked any attempt to discipline Swalwell for his indiscretion.

Good Catholic, Brother Joe Biden, has a profound appreciation for the Chinese and

Ukrainians since on more than one occasion they have given his drug and sexually addicted son, Hunter, thirty pieces of silver, which he has shared with his dad.

The republicans expelled Santos, not because he did what democrat politicians do without consequence, but because of self-destructive righteousness.

Republican politicians overcompensate for the way the media depict them, namely as mean-spirited, ultra-partisan right-wingers. They are too stupid to realize that nothing they say or do will change the media's attitude toward them.

Democrats are a serious, ruthless force that will break any rule to protect any miscreant to hold onto and expand their power. They relentlessly pursue what they want and are willing to break all the rules to achieve it.

Unlike the republican response to George Santos, democrats are not going to dump their own clowns in a spasm of moral righteousness.

Let us face the facts. They have no morals. Their lies become their truth. Republicans can fall on the sword all day long.

But democrats do not play that game.

The 105 morally vain republicans who

voted to oust Santos should have reflected on his value to the party. He had the most conservative voting record of the entire New York delegation.

His district is likely to go back to being controlled by democrats. The 105 republicans who voted to expel him did the right thing – for the Democrat Party.

CHAPTER TWENTY-TWO

"The enemy is crouching at the door" (Genesis 4:7).

In 2023, on his first day as President of Argentina, Javier Milei eliminated twelve of the country's twenty-one government ministries.

Is it any wonder that I like this guy?

It would be nice if we had a president who would amputate the useless bureaucracies that are sucking the life's blood out of our country and ambushing everything spiritual.

That will not happen. We add useless bureaucracies, do not close them.

Milei made good on his vow to take a *"chainsaw"* to both government spending and what he called his country's *"political caste."* He signed an executive order to cut the number of government ministries from twenty-one to nine.

The stats?

On the day Milei took office, Argentina was suffering 143 percent inflation and 40 percent of Argentines were living in poverty. The country had a trade deficit of more than $43 billion and a $45 billion debt to the International Monetary fund.

Stuff like that cannot be fixed overnight.

His *"Chainsaw Plan"* involves selling off state-owned companies, slashing public spending, reducing and simplifying taxes, and eliminating the various governmental agencies seen to be exacerbating the country's monetary crisis.

And he plans to adopt the U.S. dollar and shut down Argentina's central bank.

Will it work? I do not know, but I like the possibility.

Among ministries he plans to cut are Tourism and Sports; Culture; Women, Genders and Diversity; Public Works; Science, Technology and Innovation; Labor, Employment and Social Security; Education; Transportation; Health; and Social Development.

In his inaugural speech Milei, an economist, said, *"There is no money. Now is the time for austerity and tough love."*

He continued, "*We do not have margin for sterile discussions. Our country demands action, and immediate action. The political class left the country at the brink of its biggest crisis in history. We do not desire the hard decisions that will need to be made in coming weeks, but lamentably they didn't leave us any option.*

"*In the last 12 years, GDP per capita fell 15 percent in a context in which we accumulated 5,000 percent inflation. As such, for more than a decade we have lived in stagflation. This is the last rough patch before starting the reconstruction of Argentina.*"

He added, "*It will not be easy; one hundred years of failure are not undone in a day. But it begins in a day, and today is that day.*"

It is early in his presidency, so whether Milei delivers or not is yet to be seen. But it is wonderful to hear the words of someone promising less government, not more.

What we have in this country is an increasingly bloated government. In 2023, we had almost three million people in the U.S. federal workforce.

The U.S. Government consists of 392 federal agencies – nine executive offices, fifteen executive departments, 259 executive department subagencies and bureaus, sixty-six independent agencies, forty-two boards, commissions and committees and eleven quasi-official agencies.

These agencies are funded through appropriations bills passed by Congress.

A stupid question is, *"Are all these agencies necessary?"*

A correct answer is, *"Of course not."*

So, why do we have them?

Well, many are for political expediency and as hitching posts for affirmative action. These agencies are filled with affirmative action recruits who do nothing all day other than pick their noses and scratch their behinds.

Can you imagine a U. S. President taking office and slashing more than half of our federal agencies. If that happened taxpayers would not notice because most do not know these agencies even exist. They operate under radar and have no valid purpose.

And even those that have a purpose do not fulfill it, but simply serve as a reward for bozos selling their souls in support of the right candidate.

Every federal agency is loaded with nose pickers and butt scratchers who would not recognize real work if it jumped up and bit them on their posteriors.

Of course, they are not entirely at fault because most government agencies do not have any real work to do. That is why so many federal employees can *"work"* from home, so they are still playing the COVID (Chinese Communist Party) virus lockdown game.

If the government were run like a *"for-profit"* business, it would be operating with at least 90 percent fewer employees. But as it is, 90 percent of federal employees are on welfare.

As of December 2023, only about one-third of federal employees had returned to *"work"* from the pandemic lockdown. So, the government is sitting on millions of square feet of unused office space.

This is stupid.

The government owns more than 460 million square feet of office space, which costs billions annually to operate and maintain.

The federal agencies that allegedly use most of this space are the Department of State, Commerce, Justice, Transportation, Homeland Security, and Education, as well as the Social Security Administration and Environmental Protection Agency.

What is needed is an agency to protect us from these agencies, especially the EPA.

On average, 17 of 24 agencies surveyed used 25 percent or less of the available space in their headquarters buildings.

But even though they have all this empty space, the government spends more than five billion a year on leases from the private sector.

Stupid becomes stupider.

Since the pandemic, the government has spent $3.3 billion on furniture for these mostly empty office buildings.

In one of his newspaper columns, Stephen Moore wrote that one of the greatest government scandals of all time is that hundreds of thousands of federal employees, for three years now, have been getting a fulltime paycheck from Uncle Sam without showing up for work.

He wrote, *"They don't call it Club Fed for nothing.*

"The COVID scare ended two and a half years ago, and most private businesses have demanded employees show up for work...What's so special and privileged about government workers?"

Moore reports that the republicans are responding to this problem, but not democrats.

Why?

He wrote, "*Well, more than 90 percent of PAC donations from federal employee unions go to...you got it. Democrats.*"

So, employees in the private sector are back to work, whereas alleged workers in the federal sector are not. So, I think we could get by with 50 percent or more fewer alleged federal workers.

In fact, we are already doing it, but still paying them. If the financial geniuses in Congress would just cut the waste, they would not have to worry about Social Security and Medicare as a problem.

CHAPTER TWENTY-THREE

"*The enemy is crouching at the door*" (Genesis 4:7).

A trans canine woman know as Knotty Princess was banned by X (Twitter) and lost her job with *"Only Fans"* because of complaints.

She said *"Only Fans"* removed her because people kept sharing her link and saying that she has sex with dogs.

She told her 185,000 followers that there is no proof that she had engaged in sex with dogs, but several tweets posted on her account suggest otherwise.

Under pressure, she said, "*I have made a*

decision to come out. I have been with six dogs this year (2023) and only two men in my entire life."

Then, comparing herself to people who trophy hunt for animals, she said, *"You bring animals death. I bring them orgasms. I am a better alternative."*

This degenerate is a direct result of American culture's emphasis on tolerance. Americans will tolerate anything, including bestiality.

If you recall, people interviewed at LGBTQ events voice support for bestiality. And that may be a qualification for being a democrat, since they also support transgender surgeries for children and allowing grown men to use girl's bathrooms.

Knotty Princess is, obviously, qualified for one of Biden's affirmative action appointments, or for an Ivy League university presidency, or for being a police chief in a democrat-run city.

It would be easy to author a book on democrat values. All you would have after researching them would be blank pages. They are the same as Satan's values.

Democrats can embrace and be lauded for their acceptance of trans canine supporters, of which, I am sure, there must be many.

I wonder if they have a flag. My guess is that they do, and if they do, it will soon be flying over the White House. And we will soon be having a special day to honor them.

Even now these trans canine folk are among the mobs protesting Israel and glorifying Hamas.

I also wonder if Knotty Princess has a degree from Harvard and taught there. If not, surely the over-hyped school can give her an honorary doctorate for her canine research.

In the meantime, while you were worrying about personal and stupid economic stuff, the department of Health and Human Services (HHS) introduced a new gender pronoun policy.

So, forget all the unimportant stuff in the world, terrorism, etc., and focus on what is important, which is whether this new gender policy violate employee rights and lead to "*misgendering?*"

Misgendering may soon lead to jail time if Biden is reelected. He is holding off for now.

The HHS policy in question requires employees to use names and pronouns that individuals use to describe themselves, and it aims to protect employee rights and foster a discrimination free workplace.

Roger Severino, a former HHS official,

claims the policy forces employees to speak falsehoods and go against their faith, potentially impacting morale and production.

Severino, an unusual and logical Harvard graduate, said the transgender pronoun mandate will force employees to deny biological realities with their own words or face firing.

He said the new policy impacts the faith of employees and their ability to express dissent. He further said the new policy allows men who identify as women to get naked in front of female colleagues in the locker room.

"It used to be that if you allowed a man to get naked in front of a woman in the workplace that it was instantly a violation of civil rights law," Severino said. *"That's the quintessential hostile work environment, subjecting women to that. Now the policy says to women who may be uncomfortable with that situation that they're the ones who have to leave."*

He said governments cannot compel speech, and certainly cannot compel false speech.

As a country we protect the right of political dissent, but at HHS employees must pledge allegiance to the Rainbow flag, not the American flag.

Stupid, huh!

If you are wondering who heads up the HHS, it is Biden appointee Xavier Becerra, a democrat, of course, and California-born lawyer and politician.

To the best of my knowledge, he does not identify as a woman, which is a bit shocking since Biden is trying to give every transgender person an office in government.

CHAPTER TWENTY-FOUR

"The enemy is crouching at the door" (Genesis 4:7).

Abraham Lincoln said, *"Elections belong to the people. It's their decision. If they decide to turn their back on the fire and burn their behinds, then they will just have to sit on their blisters."*

Today most Americans are sitting on their blisters. And most do not like it.

You may say, *"I didn't vote for the buffoon."* But a lot of stupid people did, some for as many as one hundred or more times. Your vote counts, just not as much as someone who gets to vote as many times as they want.

If you think, *"That's not fair,"* just remember that nothing Satan has a hand on is fair, and both his hands are massaging most democrats.

But if a dimwit thinks that their stupidity in following Satan is going to benefit them, they have another think coming. Satan's the only one who benefits from those who stupidly succumb to doing his evil.

Remember the Ferguson protests back in 2014. That is when the word *"woke"* was first used. Black Lives Matter (BLM) used the word to perpetrate a lie about police shootings of blacks.

To hear them tell it, so many guiltless black men had been killed by the police that year that only women and children were left. The truth be known, eleven allegedly unarmed black men were killed by the police that year.

Statistics tell us that ninety-six police officers were killed in the line of duty that year.

A black pastor friend once told me that blacks killed more blacks each year than were killed during the entire Vietnam War.

That is easy enough to check, but people with a liberal (communist/Nazi) agenda are not interested in truth or facts. If you recall Biden said, *"We choose truth over facts."*

Shame on those of us who thought they were the same. Obviously, that is not true when discussing violent, destructive protests carried out by Black Lives Matter (BLM), Antifa, etc.

Burning, looting and even murder is, according to the media, *"mostly peaceful."* Those of us who think otherwise are labeled *"racists."*

I grew up in a segregated town, went to an all-white school, but four of my best friends were black. I did not give much thought to the separate school thing, and they did not either.

How do I know this?

They told me.

Being in segregated schools did not keep us from playing sandlot baseball or football together - or at night playing basketball on a makeshift dirt court in my parents' backyard.

And although restaurants were segregated, our home was not. My friends came into the house for cookies, Kool-Aid and to use the bathroom.

Now, admittedly, my parents were different. They may have been the only republicans in Jasper County.

At 17 years of age (in 1954), I became a pitcher for an otherwise all black barnstorming baseball team. Most of the guys on the team had played in the old American and National baseball leagues.

None of them were racists, so they treated me the way they wanted to be treated. The same could not be said for fans at the games we played in the South, Midwest and Canada. We were all subjected to racism.

Because of my views on race in the nineteen sixties, I was labeled a liberal. But because I hold those same views today, I am a conservative.

My black friends were not African Americans. They were (and are) plain old Americans, no hyphen before *"American."* Get rid of the hyphens and stick to plain old *"American"* and you get rid of lots of problems.

The word *"woke"* is no longer just a word. It has morphed into a movement that many on the left use to justify socio-political change. And the *"Wokes"* in America stupidly think all systemic injustices in society can be remedied by big government.

The future of democracy is at risk in the next presidential election. It has already been dealt a crippling blow by the fraud in the 2020 election.

"There was no fraud," democrats and media say. In their attempts to convince us that Joe Biden is a legitimate president; they contend that the 2020 election was the most secure in our history.

Really?

Now a massive number of voters are

admitting how they helped the democrats steal the election by taking advantage of mail-in-ballots.

Genuine research, not the kind democrats engage in, shows that one in five voters who submitted ballots via mail admitted that they did so fraudulently.

In fact, 21 percent of all mail-in-ballots have been confirmed to be illegal in one way or another. Democrats would have you believe this is a conspiracy theory, but the truth is that it was simply a genuine conspiracy.

And the fraudsters are more than happy to brag about how they stole the election for China Joe.

Out of the 154.6 million votes cast in the 2020 election, 66.5 million were mail-in-ballots, and researchers say at least fourteen million of those were fraudulent.

I daresay that 75 percent were fraudulent and that not one of those fraudulent votes was cast for President Trump.

Most people who hate Trump do not know why they hate him. They are just used to going to the democrat trough to feed, and they do and say what the democrats want done and said.

Some people want pandemic politics, to have the government expand and play mother hen to them. The problem is that the government is not like a mother hen. They may give you enough grain to keep you alive to vote, but they are going to keep most of the grain for themselves.

We sometimes tend to forget that the government has no money other than our money and does nothing to earn money. It spends our tax money but does nothing to produce income.

Thomas Sowell, one of my favorite writers, who is black, wrote: *"If you've been voting for politicians who promise to give you goodies at someone else's expense, then you have no right to complain when they take your money and give it to someone else, including themselves."*

Four of the goofiest women in Congress, which is saying a lot, are Alexandria Ocasio-Cortez, Ilhan Omar, Rashida Tlaib and Ayanna Pressley, known as *"the Squad."*

These women have no interest in being Americans, only in promoting their social justice docket, which is applicable to only certain ethnic groups.

The nonproductive, irresponsible and disruptive squad would best be at home in a circus or carnival instead of in Congress, but stupid people are incredibly supportive of other stupid people. So, they get a lot of attention at woke rallies, protests and from the media, which cannot discern stupidity from reality.

Exposing the stupidity of the squad is easy, but few do it. Among those who expose their stupidity regularly are Tucker Carlson Greg Gutfeld, Jesse Watters, Judge Jeanine Pirro, Shawn Hannity, Laura Ingraham and Stuart Varney.

And there are others, who are too numerous to mention.

John F. Kennedy (JFK) is a democrat hero, but if he were alive today, he would be a republican. The legacies of JFK and his brother Robert are today being rejected by Joe Biden and modern-day democrats.

JFK was a staunch Cold War anti-communist/socialist. He was for lower taxes, was pro-life, served the country valiantly in uniform, was patriotic, was a hawk protecting First Amendment civil liberties, and he and Robert took on union and government corruption with a vengeance.

How many democrats today can check those boxes?

Democrats today denounce what were their mainstream values 60 years ago. That is why it is so stupid for someone to say, *"I vote democrat because my daddy voted democrat."*

So did every member of the Ku Klux Klan in years past.

Democrats accuse republicans of being racist, but it is the Democrat Party that has always been racist.

The mystery of how democrats got the black vote is no mystery. They promised black people the moon and so far, have only given them a Moon Pie.

That did not change under Clinton and Obama, and it is sure not going to change under Biden, not unless they are a sexual deviant or worse.

And unlike daddy's democrats who wanted to lower taxes, Biden, Bernie Sanders and Elizabeth Warren want to raise them 50, 60 or 70 percent.

CHAPTER TWENTY-FIVE

"The enemy is crouching at the door" (Genesis 4:7).

As long as one Muslim is alive there can be no peace in the world. That is because Islamic ideology is an incurable cancer that spreads like a wildfire. The *Qur'an* is Satan's book of psalms, sung by a chorus of his demons, and believed by the more stupid of the world.

So, why is our government, academia celebrities, media and even religion lying about the intent of Islam? Is it because of fear of reprisal, or simply because of stupidity?

Of course, Biden and democrats are stupid about everything, so why not Islam? It is doubtful that any of them have studied the *Qur'an* or the *Hadith*, and even if some have, they are incapable of comprehending either.

The only understanding necessary from study of the *Qur'an* and the *Hadith* is that all followers of Muhammad are terrorists. They may not be in an identifiable terrorist organization, but their goal is the same as that of every Muslim — the eradication of all Christians and Jews in the world.

Muslims currently living in the United States use our laws when they benefit them, but their goal is to eventually replace them with Sharia Law.

The theme of those living in Arab-controlled countries is *"Death to America,"* and they delight in burning our flag.

Large scale, high-intensity warfare ignited by barbarians is not outdated. October 7, 2023, should have taught us that, but it obviously has not.

Hamas represents the Muslim (Islamic) mind. And with the stupidity of open borders, we have opened ourselves up to radical Islamists doing to Americans the same thing they did to Jews on October 7, 2023.

Our wonderful government seems intent on putting us in the same situation that Nazi-besieged Leningrad was in during November of 1942.

The city's population had dropped from 3.3 million to about 800,000 in just over a year. People murdered for food, to steal ration cards, or worse still to eat their victims.

You say that cannot happen here. Well, you are oh so wrong.

If you know anything about history, which most people do not nowadays, you know that on a regular basis in Savannah, Georgia bloated bodies from vessels sunk by German submarines washed ashore, and ship builders worked 24 hours a day, seven days a week, to produce Liberty Ships.

At the same time, at the Treblinka Extermination Camp, where 14,000 Jews could be murdered in a single day, there were 15 to 20 suicides a day.

Columnist George Will wrote that *"Today the desire of Hamas to complete the Holocaust is applauded by moral cretins in academic cocoons (some Princetonians chanted 'Globalize the intifada'), too uneducated to understand the grotesque pedigree of their enthusiasm."*

He continued *"...broadcast snippets of combat have drained war of its power to shock.*

"Today academic ethicists at a safe distance are instructing Israel to be 'proportionate' to what was done on October 7. Perhaps the students and faculty exhilarated by Hamas need to see pictures of what was done.

"So, give very U.S. college and university the 46-minute video that Israel compiled from Hamas cameras and other sources, showing the sadists inflicting their carnage. Challenge the schools to screen it. This would be disturbingly educational. But the schools, many of them uneasy about such things, should do it anyway."

Because of the video games students play, because of the communist indoctrination that they have received, and because most have not had a close encounter with death, I doubt that the video would change the minds and attitudes of most.

These students do not have a clue about what the future holds, and they do not want to know. It is obvious that in their classes they are not being taught about the intent of Islam.

You do not have to be a genius to understand that American academia is rotten to the core. The brainwashing done to students by a bunch of cowardly communist weenies under the guise of being teachers has been highly effective.

The professors with whom I taught in Oregon were all self-proclaimed geniuses. So, they looked with a jaundiced eye at an academic from Texas.

I listened to their political logic and tried not to laugh at what their drug-generated brain cells whipped up in what had to be a blender. They made as much sense as an onion, garlic and orange cocktail, which would have anyone with half a BB-sized brain reaching for a bottle of Listerine.

I became convinced that most of them had been participants in a CIA psychedelic experiment because most of them did not make as much sense as the patients in the novel and movie *One Flew Over the Cuckoo's Nest.*

Their primary concern was LGBTQ rights, which in Oregon already exceeds equal rights, and which today even take precedence over equal rights everywhere in America.

Following the barbarian attack on October 7, 2023, and Israel's response, some idiot college students (many of whom were Muslim) protested the retaliation by Israel. They called for the death of Israel and the Jews.

Three university presidents – from Harvard, M.I.T. and the University of Pennsylvania – justified the students call for genocide, depending on "*context*."

Just what "*context*" justifies barbarism?

Two of those presidents have been fired and the other, Harvard's head honcho and an affirmative action hire, resigned.

These three deeply mediocre presidents, all women, who have been hiding their mediocrity in alleged bastions of higher education, have with their stupidity embarrassed themselves and the schools they represent before the largest audience that they will ever have.

These schools punish faculty and students for being "*fatphobic*," using unwanted pronouns, or saying there are but two sexes but, obviously, they think it is okay to call for the genocide of an entire ethnic group that they deem the oppressor in a battle against evil that they stupidly embrace.

Beyond stupid, huh?

I do not see how they can call themselves Americans, but being an American is not particularly important to them. Being American is not important to anyone who supports the genocidal actions of the evil that permeates Islam.

In fact, Islamic extremism is marching music for *"woke"* progressives and adherents of *"critical race theory."*

Most intelligent Americans, those Hillary Clinton has referred to as deplorables, have separated themselves from such stupidity. They look at the willingness of Ivy League alumni, faculty, trustees, donors and students who are apologists for bloodthirsty barbarians, and who tolerate the politicalization of America, and say, *"These people aren't very smart."*

And they are right. The truth be known, they are downright stupid, because these demented clowns on the left are supporting an evil ideology that would sooner behead them than swat a fly.

But when you talk about stupidity, an LGBTQ protest supporting Hamas and its Muslim base takes the cake. These people are either ignorant of the Islamic attitude toward queers or have a death wish.

As a reporter, I covered a few protests,

but none like these. At my alma mater, Baylor University, protests of the Vietnam War attracted a half dozen or so people who were most often not Baylor students.

And protests of a nuclear power plant near Glen Rose, Texas, attracted fewer people than the professionally made signs that were available.

Maybe sign companies are behind protests since professional signs are always available at a moment's notice. Or maybe global warming is responsible for protests, especially stupid ones.

These protests for the eradication of Jews attract large and sometime violent people, many of whom do not have a clue about what they are protesting.

On most college campuses the only kind of protests that would draw a crowd would be one calling for the eradication of the school's football program.

At most schools, football is more important than any subject matter.

At one of the universities where I taught, football games attracted fewer people than an illegal cock fight. And some administrators complained that football was responsible for a more than million-dollar deficit at the school each year.

I asked, *"So, why don't you get rid of football?"*

The answer: *"The band would not have any place to play."*

Colleges and universities are not accountable for much of anything and thinking is prohibited, so calling for genocide of an entire people falls in the unaccountable category.

I once asked a millionaire for a gift of a million dollars for the university where I was teaching. He gave me the money but said, *"Giving money to a university is like pouring it down a hole. Next year you won't be able to tell me where a dime of it went."*

He was right, of course. When it comes to waste, education ranks right along with government. And liberal educators, along with media and government, are also experts at suppressing truth.

Only recently has the public learned that former National Institute of Allergy and Infectious Diseases Director Anthony Fauci and National Institutes of Health Director Francis Collins lied to the American public to discredit the theory that COVID was spread by a Wuhan, China lab.

It is sacrilege, of course, to think that they were doing anything more than protecting you from your ignorance. These people are so oh so brilliant that we are not to question anything they say.

So, with the help of the government and media, Americans were propagandized to believe a big lie. We were told that the accusation against the Wuhan lab was a conspiracy theory.

But a conspiracy is only a theory if it is not true.

Think for a moment about how many alleged conspiracies have been proven to be true during China Joe's tenure as President. And think about how many lies you have been asked to swallow.

If you are like me, both the alleged conspiracies and lies have left a bad taste in your mouth that is more gagging than a big dose of Castor Oil.

It is no conspiracy theory that Fauci and Collins used their control of federal funding to downplay their culpability for the millions of deaths caused by the COVID virus.

You are probably asking, *"Why do we fund dangerous research in China, Ukraine, and in the U.S.?"*

That is right. Chinese labs in America, funded by our government, have been caught doing illegal and dangerous research here.

If Fauci and Collins lived in China and had done what they did here, they would have been executed.

You might also ask, *"Why in 2024 is our military at an 80-year low?"*

You can bet that would not be the case if Trump were President.

You may not trust the Russians, but their military listed Joe Biden, Hillary Clinton, Barrack Obama and George Soros as being the main ideologists behind the plot with Department of Defense (DoD) funding to manufacture coronavirus strains in Ukraine, China and the U.S..

You can decide for yourself whether you believe them, but *"Western Elites"* and Chinese leader Xi believe them because of an open-source paper trail that comes to the same conclusion.

You can call it a conspiracy theory if you like, but most of these alleged theories have turned out to be true. The Russian military has been demanding activation of Articles V and VI of the Biochemical Weapons Treaty, which would result in a Security Council investigation and international military tribunals.

Things are not always what they seem, especially if the media is cooperating with the aggressor. The truth is that our CIA/State

Department is guilty of funding Nazi-militant groups in efforts to overthrow sovereign nations.

I do not claim to be a prophet, but I believe that one day we will be fighting alongside the Russians against Muslim hordes out to destroy the world. As to when that day will come, I do not know. But that day is a lot closer than most people think.

There are many reasons why people do not like Jesus, but the primary one is that they love evil and hate the light of goodness and peace that He brings to the world.

He is the only cure for satanic stupidity that prefers war to peace.

God is the only hope for truth, which is now being burned to a crisp on the altar of media.

Tucker Carlson said that journalism now only exists to protect the ruling liberal elites and to suppress information from us.

He said, *"Reporters no longer reveal essential information to the public; they work to hide it. Journalists act as censors on behalf of entrenched power. They have contempt for the public. They hate the truth."*

He went on to say that over the past four years reporters have hidden vital truths from the public about Russia Gate, Hunter Biden's laptop and the origin of the coronavirus.

"Democracy can't function when the press tries to manipulate elections by deciding what the public does and doesn't need to know," Carlson said. *"Voters can't know what they're voting for. People do understand they're being manipulated, and they resent it. The population becomes angry and paranoid. Things fall apart."*

Carlson said the only solution to a propaganda spiral like the one we are living through now is telling the truth about things that matter, clearly and without fear.

"With polls showing Donald Trump leading Joe Biden, the level of dishonestly emanating from the media to try and help Biden win will be off the charts," he said. *"People need trusted voices to sift through the media lies, conspiracy theories and gaslighting about Donald Trump."*

Another thing we must not forget is that DEI (diversity, equity and inclusion) are propaganda words.

CHAPTER TWENTY-SIX

"The enemy is crouching at the door" (Genesis 4:7).

Public school enrollment has stagnated. Private school enrollment has increased.

Why? Because most people send their kids to school to get an education, not to be indoctrinated by public education into thinking that communism, transgenderism and homosexuality are the cat's meow.

Perversion and anti-Americanism may be the most important things in the lives of teacher union leaders, but it is at the bottom of the totem pole for most people with a brain.

In addition to educational rot, major newspapers have folded in the world of media.

The *New York Times* and *Washington Post* got rich off Trump hatred for a while, but recently their finances have dropped faster than a ship's anchor in a thousand feet of water.

And the three major TV networks, along with CNN, MSNBC and PBS, cook up a big batch of Trump-phobia and anti-America stupidity every day.

Higher education is in even more trouble. Colleges and universities are being run by liberals who have never run anything other than their mouths.

Morally and intellectually, higher education has collapsed and now serves only as a headquarters for football teams and perversion.

Celebrities, who we did not realize were

celebrities, are handed microphones to proclaim whatever they may be thinking (questionable that they are capable of thinking) about the political landscape. And like Biden and Obama, they let their mouths overload their rear ends and come across as stupid because they do not have a script.

One of the stupider things to happen in 2023 was a global warming summit in Qatar.

Mindless environmentalists proposed ridding the planet of fossil fuels to people whose economy is built on fossil fuels.

Of course, these were not real environmentalists, just UN and other jerks like John Kerry who jumped on the global warming bandwagon for the purpose of enriching themselves, and with the hope of getting 15 minutes of fame.

Columnist John Stossel quoted Kerry as saying that *"It will take trillions of dollars to solve climate change. There is not enough money in any country in the world to actually solve this problem."*

Stossel also wrote, *"Kerry has little understanding of money or how it's created. He's a multimillionaire because he married a rich woman. Now he wants to take more of your money to pretend to affect climate change."*

Growing up in East Texas and less than one hundred miles from the coast, every summer I experienced temperatures of more than one hundred degrees, along with humidity that drenched a person's clothes in sweat.

As a teenager, I worked with an otherwise all-black logging crew cutting down cypress trees in the swampy terrain around my hometown of Jasper. The workday was daylight until dark, but we did not complain because overtime pay was $1.50 an hour.

When I was not logging in those swampy areas, slapping at mosquitos and dodging snakes, I was pulling chemically soaked timbers off the green chain at the sawmill.

The work hours were the same, daylight until dark. And again, we were grateful for the overtime pay.

After work I went home, ate supper, took a bath and went to bed. We did not have air-conditioning or a fan, but sheets made wet by humidity and an occasional breeze through open windows, along with bone-tired tired weariness, enabled me to get a few hours of sleep.

Some kids dreaded football practice in the heat of late August, but for me, even with the oppressive heat, it was a vacation.

My dad, mother, ancestral relatives and everyone else dealt with the heat in numerous ways in their day. It was much harder to deal with the cold.

As I have already mentioned, today there are twenty deaths from the cold for every death from heat. That seems to have escaped the notice of global warming addicts.

Heat kills, but so does cold – and much more so than heat. But fearmongering does not increase or reduce deaths caused by either.

We are told that sea levels have risen three feet over the past one hundred years. During the next one hundred years we are told that if we continue living as we are they will rise an estimated three inches to three feet, and that the average temperature will go up one to one and a half degrees.

The sea level and temperature will not destroy the earth and humankind. Adjustments will be made by scientists and people who know more than they know today, and things will only get greener. Transportation will be different, but not electric.

Rising sea levels certainly will not destroy the planet. Just remember that one-third of the Netherlands is below sea level, parts of it by twenty-two feet.

China, of course, is not worried about climate change. They are building new coal burning plants faster than we can shut one down. Absence of coal for heating and producing electricity in the U.S. will kill more people than global warming.

The bozos in our government cannot fix the environment. They can only give money to charlatans who say they can. And, of course, most of the allegedly elected clowns are getting a kickback.

We could do a lot to solve any alleged climate problems by getting rid of lobbyists, as well as bureaucrats who write checks to businesses that promote the climate farce perpetrated by the Biden administration.

Biden does not care if the air you breath is rancid if his air is not rancid. He does not care if you are cold, if he is warm, or if you are hot if he is cool.

He does not have to pay huge utility bills, put gas in his car, buy groceries or make a house payment. He has none of your problems, so he does not care about your problems.

And he can arrogantly declare lies and suffer no repercussions because he has stupid bottom feeder alleged journalists in his pocket.

Years ago, a reporter asked Hall of Fame football quarterback Joe Namath what he majored in when in college at the University of Alabama.

"Journalism," Namath replied. *"It's the only thing I could pass."*

Well, many of the people who call themselves journalists today could not pass a basic journalism quiz, but they certainly know how to suck up to the democrats who are in power.

Believing our current government is like believing that Santa Claus is going to come down your chimney with a sack full of goodies, or that Hunter Biden did not molest underage girls, or that the Bidens did not taken any foreign money.

Just remember that democrats accuse republicans, and especially Trump, of everything they are doing and of what they are really like.

For example, they accuse Trump of being a dictator like Hitler. That is because Biden and Obama both aspire to be dictators like Hitler. They are a mirror imagine of what Hitler was like.

So, sling that back in the faces of democrats who accuse Trump of being Hitler-like.

Anytime Trump speaks, democrat alleged reporters take it out of context. That was the case in a 2023 when Trump spoke in New Hampshire and said the criminals (called immigrants by media) were poisoning the blood of America.

During a press gaggle an AP (Associated Press) reporter asked Republican Senator J.D. Vance of Ohio to react to Trump's comments. She got more than she bargained for.

"He didn't say all immigrants are poisoning the blood of America," Vance responded. *"He said illegal immigrants are poisoning the blood of America...You guys seem far more upset about the guy who criticized the problem than about Joe Biden, who's causing the problem. Why do you think that Donald Trump's language is targeted at the blood of the immigrants and not at the blood of the American citizens who are being poisoned by the fentanyl problem?"*

Vance went on to say, *"You are allegedly a journalist. You're supposed to speak truth to power, and yet you're trying to circumscribe and narrow the limits of debate on immigration in this country. What you're doing is not speaking truth to power. You're trying to police the guy who's criticizing the problem so that Americans don't pay attention to the guy who caused the problem."*

Mainstream *"alleged"* journalists have

their noses so far up Biden's rectum, all democrat rectums for that matter, that they do not know what truth smells like.

Hitler's World War II propaganda machine has been reincarnated in American's mainstream media.

CHAPTER TWENTY-SEVEN

"The enemy is crouching at the door" (Genesis 4:7).

Massachusetts democrats are pushing for noncitizen voting. You did not need a crystal ball to see that it would come to this. Flood America with illegals (criminals), give them money and stuff attributable to democrats, and let them vote, knowing they are going to vote for Santa Claus democrats.

Whether all these illegals (criminals) know that they are being manipulated or not, they are going to vote for Santa Claus.

This is the entire purpose of open borders. And if democrats are allowed to get away with this kind of crap, we will end up being just like the third world countries from which the illegals (criminals) came.

But the democrats in power do not care. They will still be rich and powerful and have everything they want (until the Muslims take over).

About these evil perverts my dad used to say, *"They make my rectum want a dip of snuff."*

Dad, of course, used more colorful language than I do.

Democrats who want open borders are Satan's disciples, demons clothed in phony righteousness. They are no different than Hamas and the satanic perverts who support them.

Without just coming out and saying it, they seek the demise of America.

So, why not just promise everyone in the world something for voting in America's elections.

Elections were stolen in 2020 and 2022, so what makes you think they will not be stolen in 2024?

Billionaire democrats pay unethical people to criminalize the vote through harvesting and mail-in balloting. Everyone knows it, but no one does anything about it.

And take a good look at the people who are counting the vote. Would you trust them to watch your house while you are gone? Well, you are trusting them with the fate of the nation.

Every day increased evidence of criminal behavior in the 2020 election is being found.

But mainstream media is not interested in facts or the truth. So, Pinocchio pundits continue to cover up for their democrat loves like Biden and Obama.

I have tried to find out why they have this attachment to evil, but without success. The only thing I can figure is that they are children of Satan.

One in five voters who cast mail-in ballots in the 2020 election admit to participating in at least one kind of fraud. They are even proud of it, brag about it.

And less than one percent of all absentee and mail-in ballots were rejected in 2020. Every fraudulent ballot made it through our country's gaping sieve of the electoral system.

In a recent survey, eight percent of respondents admitted that a friend, family member or organization (such as a political party) offered to pay or reward them for voting.

And it is important to note that 38 percent of Biden voters submitted mail-in ballots, compared to 23 percent of Trump voters.

Strangely, or maybe not so strangely, when Biden was behind in certain states, a vast number of mail-in ballots were suddenly found, all of which were votes for him.

A few people questioned this, but democrats controlled the vote count.

CHAPTER TWENTY-EIGHT

"The enemy is crouching at the door" (Genesis 4:7).

Former President Trump wants drug and sex traffickers to get the death penalty. I do, too. I could be wrong, but think most Americans agree.

So, why do democrats oppose this?

Most people, obviously, oppose things that affect them, so how would the death penalty for drugs and sex trafficking affect democrats?

Inquiring minds want to know.

We can speculate, of course, but I do not want to accuse everyone for what some are doing. Unfortunately, our government has many elected officials and bureaucrats, both democrat and republican, who are into drugs and all sorts of sex, including pedophilia.

And only the stupid among us believes that none of these officials get money from the cartels.

There is no doubt that Satan and his minions are entrenched in D.C., just as they are in every small town and city in America. Here and abroad, they outnumber Christians by a bunch.

China, a satanic stronghold with 1.4 billion people, does not have a drug problem. It is no secret why. They execute drug dealers. This was not some moral decision on their to Part, because they have no objection to peddling drugs to other countries.

China and Mexico are the leading producers of the synthetic drug Fentanyl, and they will sell stupid Americans all they want.

You see, the Chinese understand how drug users weaken a country. And they want to weaken America even more than it has already been weakened.

Why?

It is because they plan to someday take over the USA. They are competing with Islam to do so.

We know that Mexico's Sinaloa Cartel is the leading distributor of Fentanyl in America. So, knowing that, why have we not wiped these vermin off the face of the earth. We have the personnel to do it.

As to why it has not been done, it is because the cartel is greasing the palms of key players in D.C.

For that matter, why haven't all cartels, with Mexico's blessing, been designated as terrorists by our government?

Well, the Mexican government is not going to do it. For all we know, the Mexican government may be a cartel. It certainly is not a friend to America.

President Trump said, *"You execute a drug dealer, and you save 500 lives, because they kill an average 500 people. It's terrible to say, but you look at every country in the world that doesn't have a problem with drugs, they have a very strong death penalty for the people who sell drugs."*

I do not know where Trump got that five hundred number, but I will take his word for it. In fact, if you saved only one life by executing a drug dealer, it would be worth it.

But back to Mexico. Because the Mexican government refuses to do anything about the cartels, and refuses to let us do anything about them, Mexico is responsible for more American deaths each year than any of our alleged enemies.

Nobody wants to say this, especially in our government, but Mexico is our greatest enemy.

How can I say that?

Well, the drug death toll in America in 2021 was 106,000. And every year for many years the number of deaths has been at least that many.

Contrast that statistic with our military deaths in Afghanistan over a period of 20 years. The 20-year total was 2,448 killed, along with 20,713 wounded.

You might not like my logic, but I do not see how anyone with half a BB-sized brain can think Mexico is a friend of the U.S.

In addition to killing 100,000 or so Americans each year with drugs, they are not exactly helping with our border situation. And our trade deficit with them each year is more than $100 billion.

Illegals entering the country from Mexico costs American taxpayers $451 billion or more a year, so our generosity has no boundaries.

So, what is good about our relationship with Mexico?

Absolutely nothing. As with other countries, we are the giver and Mexico is the receiver.

Biden, hat in hand, asked the Mexican President for help with the border situation. The response: *"We'll curb the 2024 migrant flood if you will aid dictatorships in Latin America."*

We need to stop asking and start demanding. Stop aid and trade and you will not need to ask.

Now the information that I have just

provided is available to our government, so why do we have alleged leaders kowtowing to Mexico?

It cannot simply because of Mexico's avocado crop.

As with everything else, there must be some dollar signs somewhere. Congressmen and senators have not gotten rich on their salaries alone.

Drug users, obviously, are participants in their own deaths, but what about the thousands of American and Mexican children who go missing every year? Their fates are often worse than death.

The cartels have discovered that human trafficking is much more lucrative than the sale of drugs. America is blanketed with pedophiles and satanic cults that pay top dollar for children to use for perversion, sacrifice and even cannibalistic practices.

You may be naïve and think this does not go on in the town or city in which you live. But it has been going on since shortly after Eve gave Adam that piece of fruit, and it has only intensified over the years.

With the advent of the Internet, smut mongers worldwide have had a field day. But they can only invade receptive minds. And there are plenty of those worldwide.

However, the kind of satanism, cultism, cannibalism and witchcraft coming across the border will curl your toes. But those bringing it are just as shocked to discover what is already here.

Some call it weirdness, I call it evil. And you must kill evil before it kills you.

In 2023 a democrat staffer for Maryland Senator Ben Cardin filmed himself having sex with another man in a room typically used by the Senate Judiciary Committee.

This was not some isolated incident. Rumor has it that numerous perverts have filmed themselves having sex in the Halls of Congress and in the White House.

So, what can you expect when you get a gold star from the president for hiring a homosexual or fly the queer flag over the White House.

Aren't you tired of playing like these people are normal, even special?

Do heterosexuals have a flag? If we do, I have never seen it. And I agree with Teddy Roosevelt. We should have only one flag in this country, the American flag.

How stupid is it to have a flag based on sexual orientation? For that matter how stupid is it to have parades based on sexual orientation?

It is stupider than stupid, goofier than goofy, and it just proves these folks are mentally ill.

It figures that Biden and Obama would want mentally ill people in government, because the two of them are well past mere mental illness. They both think they know more than God.

I have no problem with state or college flags flying alongside the American flag, but not homosexual, lesbian, transgender, Mexican, Palestinian or Israeli flags.

This is America. And yes, I believe in America first.

Regarding our healthcare problems, our government is loaded with self-proclaimed experts. So, when it comes to healthcare, even if they flunked high school biology, they think they know more than healthcare professionals.

They also cannot keep their noses out of clandestine and military operations, which they know even less about. And, of course, Biden, champion of diversity and perversion, appointed the first openly gay Secretary of the Army.

Quite a few alleged leaders at the Pentagon wear panties, bras and lipstick. I am sure that is very frightening to our enemies.

Islamists would like to get their hands on

this clown who was appointed Secretary of the Army. And all the other homos who are hiding out in our military.

One of the benefits that many of us received from joining the military was help with higher education. Now some join to get a free sex change operation.

How many of the mostly lawyers in our government know the truth about the pedophile pandemic that is sweeping our nation, or the homosexual agenda that is making us vulnerable to attack from our enemies, or the truth about climate change, government waste, or the dangers posed by China, Islam and Mexico.

They know, but they just will not accept the truth.

Every year for the past nine years, Republican Senator Rand Paul of Kentucky has released a *"Festivus"* report outlining government waste. The $900 billion he mentioned that the government might as well have flushed down the toilet in 2023 is just the tip of the iceberg.

You may not know that we allocated funds to study Russian cats on treadmills, photos of Barbies as identification to obtain COVID funds, six million dollars towards tourism in Egypt, or that your taxes gave $200 million to struggling artists like Post Malone, Chris Brown and Lil' Wayne.

And you might be surprised to know that the Department of Defense (DoD) lost $169 million of stored military gear.

Paul, who I am proud to say graduated from Baylor University, my alma mater, said, *"Who's to blame for our crushing level of debt? Everybody. This year, members of both parties in Congress voted to raise the debt ceiling, which empowered the government to borrow an unlimited amount of money until 2024. As Congress spends to reward its favorite industries and pet projects, the American taxpayers are forced to pay the price through record high inflation and crippling interest rates."*

He added, *"The same big spenders teamed up, yet again, to continue sending Americans' hard-earned money to foreign countries and funding endless wars, all while ignoring our porous southern border."*

I am sure most American taxpayers would like to read the findings of the transgender monkey research, which cost us $33.2 million.

And my guess is that a lot of those monkeys look like members of Congress.
And where did they find these transgender

moneys? My guess is in Doctor Fauci's lab, where I am guessing that they have been fed a diet of bats.

Here is another critically important issue about Labrador Retrievers that has been discovered by taxpayer-funded research. Fur color does not affect their body temperatures after a hot summer's walk.

I had wondered about this for years (sarcasm), so Congress relieved my concern by giving Southern Illinois University $1.7 billion for research.

I have no clue as to how much the *"hot dog"* research cost, but this tells us a great deal about the importance of higher education.

We should all thank God for Doctor Fauci. Under his leadership the National Institute of Allergy and Infectious Diseases (NIAID) funded a study using $477,121 to force-feminize male rhesus macaques (monkeys) in a Florida lab, critical research that flabbergasted the entire monkey world.

The experiment involved administering female hormones to these male monkeys to investigate potential vulnerabilities to HIV, even though critics argue that monkeys are not susceptible to HIV.

It is unknown if the parents of these trial money gave their consent to have their male offspring feminized. If not, we can expect some lawsuits.

Paul said there were undisclosed expenses from a $2.7 million grant for training Department of Homeland Security personnel, studying Russian cats on treadmills and meth-head monkeys, and a $3.8 million grant to create graphic novels on disinformation, and exploring COVID-19 misinformation in black and rural communities.

In December 2023, Biden claimed to have defied the Supreme Court and given 136 million people relief from school debt. This was an amazing feat (sarcasm) since only forty million people have school debt.

But coming from a democrat the $136 million figure is not surprising. California Congresswoman Maxine Waters said seven hundred billion people would lose their health insurance if Obamacare was dumped.

Amazing since the world population is only 8.05 billion.

And remember, it was Biden who also said, *"We choose truth over facts,"* showing that he is unfamiliar with the meaning of either.

This clown president thinks we should thank him for the border crisis; depleting our military and law enforcement; wrecking both the healthcare system and education; raising taxes; record high inflation; jeopardizing the nation's power grid; depleting our strategic oil reserve; wasting billions on fake global warming; suckering people into buying electric vehicles; giving billions to foreign countries, promoting anti-Americanism; kissing up to communists and fascists; the explosion in drug and human trafficking; normalizing immoral behavior and, through partisan politics, destroying faith in all governmental agencies.

So, thank you, China Joe.

The most demanding thing to do is to find something positive Biden has done.

Unfortunately, democrats are so used to lying for him that they claim every stupid thing he does is positive.

Not surprisingly, these are people of questionable intellect.

But when you have someone like actor Robert DiNiro and Adam Schiff in your corner, you have all the stupidity you can handle.

Biden has also been trying to micro-manage Israel's war against Hamas when he cannot manage anything here in America.

He keeps sending Netanyahu mixed signals about America's commitment to eliminating Hamas, possibly because he is fearful of losing the Muslim vote in America. It is stupid that we even have a Muslim in America. They are not here to be Americans. They are here to destroy America.

But democrats are opening the door into America for every Tom, Dick and Harry, no matter where they are from. All they care about is that they vote democrat, even if they are not citizens.

They should not be allowed to vote, nor should government employees.

Why do I say the latter?

Taxpayers pay government employees. Because the money they receive is taxpayer money, the fact is that they do not really pay taxes. They are simply returning a portion of taxpayer money they receive in salary.

So, they really pay no taxes on a government pension or social security when they retire. They are just returning a portion of what taxpayers provide for them.

Therefore, why should they have a vote.

Taxpayers in the private sector are the only people who should be allowed to vote. That would provide a fairer election.

But back to the Israelis and their war against Hamas, which Biden's stooges want to micromanage.

VP Harris, who cannot keep from giggling under any circumstances, said, *"Under no circumstances will the United States permit the forced relocation of Palestinians from Gaza or the West Bank, the besiegement of Gaza, or the redrawing of the borders of Gaza."*

Is that right, Kamala?

I did not know you had been made the ruler of the world.

Then there's Secretary of State Antony Blinken, a possible transgender clone of Hillary Clinton, who said that even if Israel dismantles Hamas, they should not get the credit.

And Defense Secretary Lloyd Austin, a black man who has sold out to democrat lunacy, said, *"In this kind of fight, the center of gravity is the civilian population. And if you drive them into the arms of the enemy, you replace a tactical victory with a strategic defeat."*

Wow!

Interpret, if you can, what this clown said. It is too deep for most of us.

Fortunately, Netanyahu knows that when he is dealing with Biden, and members of his troupe of clowns, that he is dealing with stupidity. So, he has made it clear that Israel will decide what is best for Israel, not a herd of donkeys in D.C.

During Obama's tenure as president, the White House's attitude toward Israel was not friendly. That is because Obama is a Muslim, educated in Muslim schools where he was taught to hate Jews.

Hatred toward Christians and Jews, and the desire to murder them, comprises most of the curriculum of an Islamic school. Obama was fully indoctrinated into that ideology.

More than 100,000 Christians are murdered by Islamists every year, and no one seems to notice. In fact, in 2023 more than 100,000 Christians were murdered in Nigeria alone.

Have you ever heard Biden or Obama make mention of this? Or the UN?

I have not.

CHAPTER TWENTY-NINE

"The enemy is crouching at the door" (Genesis 4:7).

Democrats are to the point of violence and insurrection, hell-bent on stopping Donald Trump from winning the White House.

The man, obviously, knows something about democrats that they are afraid he will expose if he is in the Oval Office.

The truth is that we all know something about them, which is that far too many of them are anti-America.

Individually, we cannot do much about it. They do not fear us since they currently control the legal system. But if Trump becomes President, they are afraid he will do something about the hog pen of communism and Nazism that they have been wallowing around in, and about the slop that the media has been feeding us.

He is likely to Roto-Rooter the sewer pipes where democrats like to hang out; and put a noose around the necks of their drug, child sex trafficking and war money sources.

He might even appoint people who would bring them to justice for their potpourri of crimes.

Tucker Carlson said, *"Democrats aren't content to leave it up to the voters to decide Trump's fate. They are, instead, deploying the entirety of the civil and criminal justice system to destroy Trump personally and financially."*

Carlson is not a lawyer, which explains why he uses common sense instead of stupidity to conclude what is and is not truth.

In December of 2023, four goofuses on the seven-member Colorado Supreme Court ruled that Donald Trump could not be on the state's 2024 primary ballot for president.

The reason: they declared him to be an insurrectionist, who allegedly tried to overthrow the government on January 6, 2020.

These far-left justices (laughable) handed down their edict based on nothing but their partisan bias.

The lies democrats and their media allies have spread about January 6, threatens our democracy. But democrats could care less about democracy.

Donald Trump has never been put on trial for insurrection, or convicted of that crime, which the 14th Amendment mandates must occur before he is banned from holding office.

Carlson was one of the first media voices to call the Colorado clowns out for their lies.

He questioned, *"Donald Trump's name cannot appear on the state's ballot next fall? The four liberal judges who concluded this cited as their justification Article three of the 14th Amendment, which was written in 1868 to keep former Confederate officials from holding office. That was the sum of their reasoning, even though Donald Trump has never been convicted by any court of insurrection."*

Carlson factiously further questioned,

"And although the 14th Amendment specifically does not apply to the presidency, Donald Trump cannot run for president because he's an insurrectionist?"

Some world leaders see this ruling as the United States acting just like the Communist Chinese in banning political opponents from challenging the sitting leader. They have also concluded that America has lost its moral authority to lead.

Our moral authority went up in smoke when Obama was elected and has become nothing more than a pile of ashes under Biden.

Nayib Bukele, President of El Salvador (of all places) thinks America has lost its moral compass. Bukele has reduced the murder rate in his country by 50 percent after deploying the police and law enforcement to crack down on violet gangs.

Any chance that Biden will crack down on Black Lives Matter (BLM), Antifa, MS-13, the Mexican cartels or the deluge of criminals crossing our border is about as likely as me winning the lottery when I never buy a ticket.

Bukele has called out Biden for opening the southern border and creating an illegal immigration crisis, which is harming his country as well as ours.

The fact is that the U.S. has lost its ability

to lecture any country about democracy. Partisan judges vetoing the opposition party's candidate is not democracy, it is tyranny.

It is not Donald Trump who is threatening democracy. Democrats are. Their blind rage at the thought of Donald Trump sitting in the Oval Office is what is pushing America toward authoritarianism.

Carlson said, *"None of this seems very American. All of it looks like the actual end of democracy."*

In December of 2023, Netanyahu provided a solution to the war against Hamas. It was simple: 1) end Hamas; 2) demilitarize Gaza; and 3) deradicalize the Palestinians.

The first part might prove difficult since Hamas is a proxy of Iran, which has no interest in ever ending hostilities with Israel.

I do not think they will ever quit supplying Hamas, not only with weapons of war but also, if necessary, with personnel.

The only way to demilitarize Gaza is to make it a part of Israel, and to rid it of all alleged Palestinians.

Netanyahu's third part of a solution is to deradicalize Palestinians, which would involve stopping imams from teaching hatred of Jews in schools.

That certainly is not going to happen.

It cannot happen if there is one *Qur'an* in the world, or one person who believes it. You cannot kill an ideology unless you kill everyone who subscribes to it.

If you are wondering why republicans vote with democrats on some of the stupidest stuff going, Tennessee Republican Congressman Tim Burchett has the one-word answer - blackmail.

There is a lot of sexual stuff going on among legislators, stuff they do not want anyone to know. Unfortunately for them, their colleagues do know about their sexual escapades, including those with minors and same sex partners, so they are extorted to vote for certain bills if they do not want their indiscretions known.

Isn't it good to know that the sex life of legislators determines what your taxes pay for or do not pay for?

Oh well, so much for representing the people. Get the goods on enough bedfellows and you can get any bill passed, no matter how stupid it is.

Government bureaucrats also make decisions for us based on their sexual indiscretions, and this year will be receiving a sizable increase in pay, for which they will repay Biden in the voting booth.

Any doubt (sarcasm) about who they will be voting for?

This is just more coal on the fire as to why they should not be allowed to vote.

With the Biden administration everything is about race and sex, and I mean all kinds of sex, including bestiality. If you are a person of color who engages in weird sex, China Joe has a place for you.

But if you are white and normal, your chances for government employment and advancement are slim to none.

If you are white and a republican or independent, you are a racist and fascist. The democrat playbook about this is straight out of *Mein Kompf* and the *Communist Manifesto*.

In fact, the democrats could teach Vladimir Putin a thing or two about *"real communism."*

Communism, Islamism, fascism and Nazism are flourishing in America's higher education. As to why, it all revolves around money, underwritten by stupidity and apathy.

Trust? You cannot trust anyone in higher education, or even at the kindergarten level. Some elementary school administrators expose kids to drag queen shows and Satanic clubs, the intent being one in the same.

They want to promote satanism and

homosexuality as this wonderful and sought-after lifestyle, and Satan as the savior/leader for which the entire world has been waiting.

Why? I am sure you know why. And you know it goes beyond liberalism and progressivism.

Why do queers and lesbians run for school board positions and hideout in plain sight as teachers and school administrators?

You know why.

These people are as much a danger to our freedoms as a stupidly sex-oriented Congress and administration.

And do you really want a battalion of homosexuals and transgenders standing between you and a horde of Islamic murderers' intent on cutting off your head?

The greatest danger to these administrator and teacher pre-college airheads in public schools is the dreaded school choice voucher, giving parents and students a chance to escape a curriculum that has been dumbing down kids for years.

There are many great administrators and teachers in public schools that have not surrendered to the Satanic evil that permeates public education, but it only takes a few bad apples to infect and rot an entire basketful.

If ethical and moral people would run for

school boards, we would still have problems in public schools because of government interference.

I had a great public-school education, but that it was pre-Lyndon Baines Johnson's *"War on Poverty."*

Back then American were lifting themselves out of poverty. The poverty rate was going down every year.

Progress in Johnson's war stopped after about seven years and $27 trillion dollars.

Columnist John Stossel explains why: *"Government's handouts changed people's thinking. They taught millions of Americans; you are entitled to a check."*

Individual responsibility went out the window. Individual responsibility became government responsibility.

"People became dependent on handouts." Stossel wrote. *"Government rarely teaches people to be self-sufficient; handouts encourage you to be helpless."*

He said, welfare created something that had never been seen in America; a near permanent *'underclass.'*

"Welfare told parents; don't get married; you'll lose benefits. Don't work; your check will be reduced. Above all, make sure the father is not home when a welfare worker

comes. If he is, your check may be reduced or eliminated."

Stossel said the government changed incentives that had motivated parents for generations, and not for the better. The result has been ruinous for millions of children.

I went to a segregated school (white teachers only) and got a great high school education, classes superior to the cream puff courses at Ivy League schools like Harvard.

My black friends – Arthur Neal, Biscuit, Capjack and Iron Man – also went to a segregated school (black teachers only) and received a high school education equivalent to mine.

Teachers in both schools were more concerned about educating us than about unions and political affiliation.

I am not advocating segregated schools, so do not understand the need for black colleges, but not white colleges. Black colleges seem racist to me.

The only reason there are more white racists in America than black racists is because whites outnumber blacks.

Percentagewise, white and black racists are about even. Most people want to just get along and be left alone.

Racism can be further reduced by

eliminating the politicians who prmote most of it.

As for so-called higher education, many colleges and universities have sold their souls to Middle East (aka Muslim) donors, so fear offending them. This has become obvious from all the recent pro-Palestinian anti-Israel rhetoric emanating from them.

These alleged institutions of higher learning allow people with Satan-twisted ideologies to determine what they think, and there is not a whole lot of thinking going on.

Universities have received billions in gifts from foreign potentates. It is no secret why these people gift universities. And it is not because they have a commitment to education. What they are doing is buying influence.

There was a time when professors taught subject matter. Now many of them just teach their biases, which amount to brainwashing and propagandizing their students with stupid ideologies and politics.

And the fact that these ideologies have in the past brought nothing but disaster to their believers does not matter, nor have their partisan politics brought great enlightenment.

Far too many of these professors ride sidesaddle, which indicates that they are not exactly mentally stable.

Did you know that a survey showed that 63 percent of adults under forty did not know that six million Jews were killed in the Holocaust? In fact, 10 percent said they had never heard the word "*Holocaust*."

During World War II the Nazis had more than 40,000 death camps and ghettos, yet more than half those surveyed could not name one.

If this does not tell us anything else, it should tell us that the teaching of history in all schools needs to be upgraded. But that would have to be done at schools that do not accept donations from foreign countries with agendas.

And it might be hard to find one of those.

For example, the Chinese have been big contributors to some of our universities as well as to the Bidens. Unless you are over the cliff stupid, you know they do not have America's best interests in mind.

CHAPTER THIRTY

"The enemy is crouching at the door" (Genesis 4:7).

That was then. This is now.

Now the doors are wide open.

Ever since he was bounced out of Heaven, Satan has walked back and forth across the earth. But there was a time in America when most doors were closed to him. That time has passed. Now most doors are open to him and closed to Christ.

That is the real crisis in America, the rejection of Jesus Christ and Scripture. Jesus and the Bible have been traded in for sexual perversion of the worse kind.

Homosexuals have been given complete freedom by our government to be in charge on what is, and is not, normal sex. And compared to America today, Sodom and Gomorrah were nothing more than play areas for adolescents.

Our Congress, the White House and judicial system have traded ethics and truth for one-night stands of sexual perversion that would shame the horniest of pigs.

We cannot clean up drugs and child sex trafficking in this country until we clean up government, which enjoys the stench and bizarre behavior coming from the bowels of hell.

God is the answer, but satanic government is hellbent on blocking Him at every turn. How long is He going to let this sexual circus continue before turning His wrath on us?

I do not know, but He, obviously, is a lot more patient than I am.

Put a bounty on these drug dealers and child molesters, let some good old southern boys chase them down and administer a little frontier justice, and our drug and child sex trafficking problems would be solved in a matter of days.

Give these same guys immunity and they will close the border for us. And let them police pro-Palestinian protests in the U.S. and the protesters will be catching flights back to the cesspools they came from.

But it is not just the government that is soft on sin; it is also academics, celebrities, churches, education and media.

Pope Francis has become a poster boy for descension among Catholics for his edict to permit church blessings on same-sex couples. The Pope is the alleged Vicar of Christ, but many Catholics see him as the Vicar of Satan.

I am not a Catholic but have many Catholic friends who think Francis will burn in hell for defying what Scripture teaches about homosexuality.

I question why the Vatican is treated as a country where America has an embassy, and why the Vatican also has its own bank.

Surrendering to homosexuality is not the first stupid move Pope Francis has made, which is why Catholic bishops all over the world are opposing him and refusing to provide church blessings on same-sex couples.

So, the Pope's declaration is likely to create a permanent split in the Catholic Church. The homosexual issue has already caused a split in the Anglican and Methodist churches, and to a much smaller degree among Baptists.

Is there anything stupider than defying the Holy Scriptures? Yet there have always been those who thought they were smarter than God.

That is certainly the case in America today, and nowhere is it any more pronounced than among the clergy.

The Pope's endorsement of gay couples should please the White House, where the homosexual agenda has been actively promoted by the Obamas and Bidens.

The *Daily Mail* reported that on two occasions Jill Biden's former Press Secretary Michael LaRosa had tried to bring his homosexual dates to his hotel room when Joe Biden was staying in the same facility.

Even though the Bidens, obviously, have no objection to homosexual behavior by their staff, this was a definite no-no and breach of security protocol.

Because Biden, an alleged good Catholic,

has fully embraced homosexuality, so firing LaRosa for simply having fun must have hurt the president deeply.

LaRosa took a few shots at China Joe in response to being fired, but remains loyal to the Democrat Party, as do most LGBTQ advocates and participants.

But as Louisiana Republican Senator John Kennedy said, *"Biden is more fixated on transgender breastfeeding than national security."*

And Alabama Republican Senator Tommy Tuberville said, *"President Biden has prolonged the Ukraine War in order to give democrats and their media allies plenty of cover to distract working class Americans from the revelations being uncovered every day through the investigations into his family's alleged influence-peddling scheme."*

Tuberville, who sits on the Senate Armed Services Committee, said that just three months into the conflict Ukrainian President Zelensky and Russian President Putin had worked out a deal that would have seen the conflict end peacefully with Russia simple reacquiring some land that was previously part of the Soviet Union.

"But that was a deal Biden, former British Prime Minister Boris Johnson, and the

rest of the global ruling class elites simply couldn't allow to happen," Tuberville said.

And if you think Biden would not allow hundreds of thousands of people to be killed to cover up his family's crimes, go to the head of the stupid line.

One of the *"woke"* extremist religious cult's primary commandments is to *"never let a serious crisis go to waste."*

Joe Biden is desperate to cover up his misdeeds and failures, and you had better believe that he is willing to sacrifice you and me to do it.

Wars, no matter where they are fought, are moneymakers for self-proclaimed elites. They have the power to start wars and the power to stop them. Many innocent people are sacrificed in the process of proving their self-importance.

The only time I ever saw my mother lose her cool and curse a man to the point where he was groveling was when I was nine years old. World War II had just ended. My dad, who was with the 28th Infantry Division, the most casualty-ridden in World War II, had received three Purple Hearts and a Bronze Star, and we were looking forward to him coming home.

We were in town to buy groceries and this guy said he had hoped the war could go on a few more months because he was doing so well financially.

By the time my mother got through with him, before a cloud of witnesses I might add, mostly church folks, he was wishing he had not let his mouth overload his rear end.

Being cursed out by a person who normally did not curse left a lasting impression on him and those who heard the verbal tongue lashing.

People who have not personally experienced war, or who have not had a loved one killed in war, relegate it to being like a 90-minute movie or a video game.

For them, it is all make-believe.

But it's not make-believe for those who must fight in the war, or their families, or for those who live in the zone where the conflict is taking place.

But if you think that the Bidens or Obamas, or that many of your elected officials and government employees, care about the blood and tears shed by others in war, you are sadly mistaken.

They only care about the money.

Like the man my mother confronted, they only care about how war benefits them.

Biden would gladly sacrifice you and your entire family for another four years (or for however long he lives) in the White House, as would Obama for another four years of pulling the strings of his puppet.

Trump has been one of the few presidents committed to stopping unnecessary wars, yet he is the one that democrats accuse of being like Hitler.

But if a democrat wants to see an image of Hitler, all they should do is look in the mirror, or look at the Biden or Obama.

If you have given any real thought to the Russian-Ukraine War, you must have questioned why Biden is so intent on giving Zelinsky, at American taxpayer expense, billions of dollars to keep it going.

But there really has never been anything secretive about it to inquiring minds. It is simply part of the greatest coverup in American history.

Some wars are, of course, justified. For example, Israel's war against Hamas, which is not a country but rather a terrorist ideology.

If Biden wants a war, let it be against terrorists like the Mexican cartels and Islamic terrorists. They are the ones killing our people, not the Russians.

During the Hamas attack on Israel October 7, 2023, these *fighters* (so called by the media; I call them cowards) raped Israeli women, drove nails into their thighs and genitals, stabbed them in the back, cut off their breasts and played with them, tossing them back and forth to each other.

If you think this is Israeli propaganda, the video evidence of this taking place came from body cams born by dead and captured Hamas cowards.

You will not see videos of the violence and torture enacted on defenseless Israeli woman at pro-Palestinian protests, but this is the culture being brought to America by Muslims.

Hamas was not content to merely execute Israelis. They burned, mutilated and decapitated their bodies.

There is a video of Israeli Gal Abdush's body splayed on the floor, legs wrenched apart, vagina exposed and covered with burns.

Her husband was also slaughtered.

Whether you like it or not, Hamas, or cowardly Islamic terrorists just like them, are coming to your town, invited by our stupid government.

This is the same government that wants to take our guns so that we will be defenseless. This is the height of stupidity.

Evey man, woman and child of age should be armed. The fate of our republic depends on it.

EPILOGUE

"The enemy is crouching at the door" (Genesis 4:7).

It is impossible to expose all the stupidity that is allowed to go on in America and the world in one book. Each stupid thing has many tentacles.

We could begin with drug and human trafficking cartels, terrorist organizations, environmental exploitation, online child exploitation, genocidal campaigns, organized crime syndicates, educational failure, political corruption, cybercrime and identity theft, religious extremism, human rights violations in conflicts, child soldier recruitment, exploitive sweatshops, or misinformation.

There are a lot of enemies that need to be confronted, and only a small number of people to confront them.

Will you be one of us?

One of the stupidest shows on TV is *The View*, daily viewed by only 2.4 million irrational women, but it may well be America's biggest source of misinformation.

None of the hosts show any inclination of having given any serious thought to issues, if, indeed, they are capable of serious thought.

Your safety in a USA under Biden has sparked many responses across social media platforms and beyond. The threats to our safety have increased significantly since he took office.

FBI Director Christopher Wray says law enforcement is more prepared than ever before but given the FBI's partisan support of democrats and its attempts to discredit Trump, that is hardly reassuring.

The top echelon of the FBI continues to serve as Biden's personal Gestapo organization. You are right to distrust the FBI because it has become a tool of the presidency, not American citizens.

The entire world is less safe since Biden took office. The number of stupid national security problems caused by Obama and Biden are too numerous to mention.

If you hate the U.S. and want to kill as many Americans as possible, an open border and kissing up to Mexico, China and the Muslim world is a good start.

So, stay vigilant because China Joe and his cohorts are going to continue letting as many illegals into the country as they can.

As for Wray, he lied to Congress, but the legislators consider that normal, because that is mostly what they do.

When Wray or any of Biden's administration ponders a question, it is because they are trying to decide whether to lie or not. And it is normally not a 50/50 proposition.

They normally opt to lie.

When terrorists hit their targets here, we will know who to blame, but the democrats will, obviously, blame Trump.

Biden's presidency poses a direct threat to the nation's welfare. Terror levels are always in a state of flux, but democrats oversimplify global terror dynamics.

I reiterate, we need to stop aiding countries that hate us. Billions are being wasted abroad while the economy in the homeland suffers.

Most of our financial problems could be solved if we stopped illegal immigration, stopped sending money to foreign countries, and stopped financing endless wars.

As for elected officials like Alexandria Ocasio-Cortez, Ilhan Omar, Ayanna Pressley, Rashida Tlaib, Jamaal Bowman, Cori Bush, Greg Casar and Summer Lee, all of whom hate America, let us buy them a one-way ticket to wherever they envision as Utopia.

These self-idolizing people, along with many others who ridicule America, need a taste of what their countries of choice are really like.

One of the cancers we could get rid of in this country is the United Nations. There is nothing *"united"* about these leeches. Every stupid thing they produce sucks the life out of America.

There are good reasons our Saudi 9/11 terrorist friends did not crash into the UN Building. Their sponsors are aware that the UN can do more harm to America in one session than dozens of planes crashing into buildings.

The UN is better at starting wars than stopping them, and better at voting for America to engage in all sorts of stupidity rather than stopping it.

Every American dime spent to maintain the UN is a dime best spent elsewhere.

And America has no financial problem that cannot be attributed to government misspending.

Good examples are Biden's government-mandated pipedream of everyone switching to electric vehicles, when most people do not want an electric vehicle.

And there is also the global warming hoax that is eating up our taxes.

A law needs to be passed based on Howard Buffet's logic. Anytime there is a deficit of more than three percent of GDP, all sitting members of Congress should be ineligible for reelection.

The core of Buffet's plan is accountability. Currently, there is none.

There is no chance of Vivek Ramaswamy being our president, but he outlined ten points for a strong America, which I think Trump will agree with.

1) God is real.
2) There are only two genders.
3) The continuance of humans flourishing requires fossil fuels.
4) Reverse racism is racism.
5) An open border is no border.
6) Parents alone should determine the education for their children.
7) The nuclear family is the greatest form of governance known to humankind.
8) People are lifted from poverty by capitalism.
9) There are only three branches of government, not four.
10) The U.S. Constitution is the strongest guarantor of freedom in the history of the world.

I make no apology for saying that America comes first with me, nor am I hesitant to say that the democrats are the party of fascism, racism, low expectations and hate. And LGBTQ activism is like a satanic cult.

You can call me a conspiracy theorist all day long, but I know the illuminati is real, and that trillionaire banker Lord Rothchild is its leader.

Nancy Pelosi
Chucky Schumer
Gavin Newsome
Adam Schiff
Eric Swalwell
Maxine Waters

Jesus is the only antidote for stupidity